Non-fiction Writing

SCAFFOLDS

Written by
Trevor Hancock

Teachers' Resource Book

HOPSCOTCH
EDUCATIONAL PUBLISHING

Published by
Hopscotch Educational Publishing Ltd
Unit 2
The Old Brushworks
56 Pickwick Road
Corsham
Wiltshire
SN13 9BX

01249 701701

© 2003 Hopscotch Educational Publishing

Written by Trevor Hancock
Series design by Blade Communications
Cover illustration by Kirsty Wilson
Illustrated by Dave Burroughs
Printed by Athenaeum Press Ltd, Gateshead

ISBN 1-904307-29-9

Trevor Hancock hereby asserts his moral right to be
identified as the author of this work in accordance
with the Copyright, Designs and Patents Act, 1988.

Year 5

Non-fiction writing
SCAFFOLDS

CONTENTS

INTRODUCTION

Non-fiction Writing Scaffolds Year 5 is intended for use in schools to help teach children how to write effectively in a variety of non-fiction genres. It improves children's ability to organise their writing so that it has purpose by familiarising them with a system of planning which they can apply to any title. As they work through the units, the children assemble a portfolio of non-fiction texts containing genre-specific vocabulary and writing features. The chosen text types coincide with those in the Literacy Framework's text-level objectives.

Many non-fiction texts are essentially cross-curricular. Thus the ability to write specifically and purposefully about a subject will benefit other areas of study.

Each unit includes information and activities on at least one sentence-level objective. Therefore the book also enhances the children's knowledge of grammar, punctuation and style.

THE PROGRAMME CONTAINS:

a teachers' book comprising:

- notes for teachers on the genres
- a bibliography for each genre
- copies of exemplar texts together with teaching notes
- guidance on how to develop grammar and punctuation skills in children's writing
- guidance on how to write in the particular genre and on specific features of each non-fiction text.

a resource book of photocopiable material comprising:

- illustrated versions of the exemplar texts especially produced for children
- notes for the children on understanding the grammar and punctuation (optional reference material)
- photocopiable activity sheets to reinforce the grammar and punctuation (optional)
- notes and tips for the children on writing non-fiction texts (optional reference material)
- differentiated scaffolds which give the children choices and guide them through the course of the text they are about to write
- vocabulary banks for them to use and add to.

HOW TO USE THE PROGRAMME

1. After examining texts in the target genre, read and discuss the exemplar text with the children, using the notes in the margin to highlight the examples of the unit's teaching point and writing feature. The children should follow the text using their own illustrated version from the resource book.

2. Next, read through and explain the 'Understanding the grammar and punctuation' section of the unit. The children can do the activities together, either orally or using whiteboards, or independently on paper.

3. Then explain the 'Helpful hints' and 'Writing features' sections of the unit to the children.

4. Read through the scaffolds with the children. Then give them the differentiated word banks and ask them to record their own vocabulary suggestions in the space provided.

5. Give the children time to plan, write and edit their non-fiction text. Each child can then store the best copies in a writing folder.

NOTES

When using the scaffolds, give the children strict time limits to plan and write each of the sections. This will give them practice in writing timed non-fiction texts as preparation for the Key Stage 2 writing test.

However, the system is entirely flexible. The activities in each unit, from reading the exemplar to composing their own text using the scaffolds, can be used in shared or guided time, with the children working collaboratively or individually.

The order of activities for each unit corresponds exactly with the sequence for the teaching of writing outlined in Grammar for Writing (DfEE 0107/200). First the model can be discussed and its grammatical and thematic features interrogated during shared reading. Next the grammar and punctuation activities can be undertaken to reinforce the children's understanding of the relevant sentence-level objectives. The helpful hints section, scaffolds, and vocabulary banks support the teacher and children in shared writing sessions and in subsequent guided and independent writing.

The method works well with children of all abilities and with bilingual pupils, as it offers the security of a detailed framework and a bank of appropriate vocabulary together with the challenge of a grammar and writing features component for each unit.

The units fulfil the text-level and sentence-level requirements of the NLS Framework for Year 5 and revise components from Year 4, many of which feature in the Key Stage 2 tests. The following units may be used specifically in literacy lessons or they may be linked with work in other curriculum areas and used accordingly.

TERM 1

UNIT 1
Genre: Recounts – historical event (T24)
Grammar: 1st and 3rd person account (S8); past tense and active verbs (S8, S9)
Punctuation: dashes (S6); connectives (S3)
Writing features: Recounts based on historical event (T24). Written in the past tense and in chronological order.

UNIT 2
Genre: Recounts – personal experience (T24)
Grammar: nouns; agreement between nouns, and verbs (S2)
Punctuation: direct and reported speech (S5)
Writing features: Recounts based on personal experience (T24). Written in form of informal letter. Organised into paragraphs.

UNIT 3
Genre: Instructional text (T25, 26, 27)
Grammar: present tense, imperative form (S8, S9)
Punctuation: use of colon (S6)
Writing features: Gathering information and taking notes (T26); contains diagrams/illustrations.

TERM 2

UNIT 4
Genre: Non–chronological report (T22,26,27)
Grammar: passive verbs, present tense (S8)
Punctuation: paragraphs to organise similar topics (T14)
Writing features: Planning, composing, editing and refining non-chronological reports (T22).

UNIT 5
Genre: Non–chronological report (T22, 23)
Grammar: pronouns (S4, S10)
Punctuation: complex sentences (S8)
Writing features: Comparing and contrasting. Acknowledging sources (T23)

UNIT 6
Genre: Explanatory text (T22)
Theme: how something works/happens (processes, systems, operations) in the natural world
Grammar: passive voice; use of cause and effect linking words (if, when, then, why, consequently); commas within sentences (S9)
Punctuation: paragraphs
Writing features: Organisation methods – introductory statement followed by series of logical steps. Includes glossary.

TERM 3

UNIT 7
Genre: Persuasive writing (T19)
Grammar: adapting writing for appropriate audience (S2); powerful verbs; adjectives
Punctuation: exclamation marks
Writing features: Using persuasive language. Using illustrations and slogans to persuade.

UNIT 8
Genre: Persuasive writing (T17)
Grammar: prepositions (S3)
Punctuation: apostrophe for possession (S5)
Writing features: Writing letters to put a point of view (T17). Arguing the case for a point of view and using evidence and reasons to persuade.

UNIT 9
Genre: Discussion text (arguments for and against) (T18)
Grammar: connectives to link clauses within sentences (S7)
Punctuation: use of paragraphs; punctuation in longer more complex sentences (S4, S6)
Writing features: Presenting arguments and information from differing viewpoints (T18)

Air Raids during the Second World War

Alfred Mason, born July 14th, 1929, can remember vividly, as if it was yesterday, the air raids over London, where he lived with his mother and older brother, Tom. His father was off fighting somewhere in Africa so they had to look after themselves. The German air force began to bomb London and other large British cities in September 1942. This sustained attack became known as the Blitz (a shortened version of the German word Blitzkrieg, which means 'lightning war') and caused terrible devastation to factories, shops and homes. The raids were usually during the hours of darkness and went on night after night.

The government and local councils did many things to try and protect ordinary families like Alfred's and their property. One of the first things they did was to set up ARP committees. ARP stood for Air Raid Precautions. These committees organised teams of wardens whose job was to: sound the air raid siren, help people get to the shelters and provide emergency help when needed. Leaflets were sent to every home giving advice on what to do if there was a raid, and how to black out the windows of buildings. Alfred remembers his mother reading it to him and discussing what they must do. Tom, being the tallest, had the job of fixing blankets, which had been dyed black, to all the windows in the

house. Alfred had to make sure a bucket of sand and a bucket of water were always ready by the back door in case the house caught fire. Although Alfred didn't realise at the time, they would have been of very little use if there had been a real fire. It was probably his mother's way of making them feel safer. Everyone was issued with a gas mask which they had to carry with them at all times. People would get into terrible trouble with the warden if he spotted someone without it.

Alfred remembers that it was very difficult going to sleep at night knowing that any time during the night an air raid might begin. They were given advance warning of a raid through the sounding of the air raid siren. This made a loud wailing sound that could be heard over a large area, and when people heard it they would stop what they were doing, even if they were at work, and quickly go to the nearest shelter. Alfred's nearest shelter – the local tube station – was large and always crowded with men, women and children. There was barely room for everyone, and the conditions in the shelter were not very pleasant. The very first time Alfred went into the shelter he just had to come out again because he felt sick. It was so dark you could hardly see anything and the smell was awful. There were thousands and thousands of people lying head to toe, all along the platform and with no facilities. At the beginning of the Blitz there were only four earth buckets down the far end behind screens that were used as toilets. Alfred felt terribly sorry for the old people because they were obviously terrified. They'd usually come down in their pyjamas and dressing gowns and they would sit up all night huddled together.

Later, things got a bit better organised and the platforms had mattresses on them. The first to arrive at least had some comfort but late arrivals would often have to try and sleep on the escalators. Eventually bunks were built along the platforms, and boilers and ovens provided so everyone could have hot food and drinks.

What Alfred remembers the most about being in the shelter was the noise coming from above ground – it was deafening and very frightening. There was the constant drone of the enemy aircraft flying above London, combined with the rapid firing of the anti-aircraft guns. But the most terrifying sounds of all were those of the explosions as the bombs landed and of the buildings collapsing. People never knew if it was their street, or even their house, that had been hit. All they knew was that some poor souls would not see daybreak, and they thanked God that they, at least, were safe.

Children (often frightened and crying) would huddle close to their mothers. Old couples would hold hands and put on a brave face, so as not to upset the children. They would cheer everyone up by telling jokes, singing and gossiping with anyone around them. There was many a time when people sat next to complete strangers but by morning they were good friends.

Everyone would stay in those crowded shelters until the air raid siren sounded again to signal that the raid was over and it was safe to leave the shelters. Often the raids would last all night and it wasn't until daybreak that people could leave, unsure of what they would find when they emerged from the dank darkness of the underground. The terrible devastation caused by the falling bombs was like a scene from a nightmare. Buildings would be on fire or smouldering; collapsed buildings were strewn across the streets in piles of bricks and concrete. ARP wardens, firemen, ambulance men and women searched through the ruins for the dead and any survivors. Ambulances and fire engines had to pick their way carefully through the rubble. People often found it difficult even to find their street because there was so much damage. It must have been like walking through a strange ghost town. Sometimes whole streets of houses were destroyed, or an unlucky few would be razed to the ground surrounded by homes undamaged by the explosions. Then the street would look like a row of teeth with some missing.

Not everyone, however, lived near a public shelter like Alfred's family did, so they had to find shelter at home. Many homes, like Alfred's Aunty Anne's had their own kind of shelter called an Anderson shelter. These were provided by the government and had to be erected in the garden by the people who lived in the house.

An Anderson shelter

Alfred recalls going to his Aunty Anne's with Tom and his mother to help them build their Anderson shelter. It was made from sheets of corrugated iron and held up to six people. They built it in the garden, after they had dug a hole for it, covered it with soil then placed sand bags around the entrance which was just a piece of sackcloth. Alfred later found out that over two million of these shelters were built. They often flooded and the local fire brigade would have to pump them out. Families would make sure that there were supplies kept in them at all times because they never knew when they might need to use the shelter.

Alfred's cousin Colin told him that Aunt Anne always made sure that everything was ready in the shelter, just in case. Oil was put in the hurricane lamp; the beds were always made; and she made sure there was a change of clothing in the clothes cupboard and that there was a supply of books and games.

These shelters were unlikely to give complete protection if a bomb exploded on top of one, but were effective even when bombs exploded nearby.

One day Alfred had gone to stay with his Aunt and they were about to settle down for tea when the air raid siren went off, and almost as soon as it stopped they heard loud banging and crashing and the sound of exploding bombs. The bombs were close and the house began to shake and his aunt hurriedly got them downstairs and into the back garden and into the shelter. The explosions got closer and dust and grit started to find their way into the shelter past the cloth doorway. The raid was a short one and they emerged to find that the house next door had partly collapsed, and part of the wall of his aunt's house was missing, exposing the kitchen to the open air!

Whichever kind of shelter people were able to use, the experience of an air raid was very frightening. It was only the steadfast spirit of everyone that enabled them to cope with this almost nightly occurrence. Despite the devastation and the loss of lives, Alfred's family never gave up and always believed that Britain would win the war.

Understanding the grammar and punctuation

First and third person

When someone writes an account of something that happened to them they write it in the first person. The writer uses pronouns such as:

I, me, mine, myself, we, us, ourselves and *our*

When someone writes an account of the experiences of someone else they write in the third person. The writer uses pronouns such as:

he, she, it, his, hers, they and *theirs*

Connectives

Clauses and sentences can be joined by adding a connective (a word that joins the two together).

Connectives are often conjunctions – *but, when, because.*

An account of events in the order they happened will use connectives that show the passage of time. For example:

just then, meanwhile, later, then, next and *after*

They built it in the garden, *after* they had dug a hole for it, covered it with soil then placed sand bags around the entrance which was just a piece of sackcloth.

Commas, brackets and dashes

Commas can be used to provide a pause in the sentence.

Although Alfred didn't realise at the time, they would have been of very little use if there had been a real fire.

Dashes and brackets can be used to give the reader more information.

Alfred's nearest shelter - the local tube station – was large and always crowded with men, women and children.

Children (often frightened and crying) would huddle close to their mothers.

Conjunctions

These simple sentences can be expanded by adding a conjunction at the beginning. Complete each sentence with your own ideas.

1. *I enjoy playing outside.*

   Whenever I enjoy playing outside, _____

2. *Sharon is a good footballer.*

   Although Sharon is a good footballer, _____ .

3. *The class worked quickly.*

   Once the class worked quickly, _____

4. *Disneyland is a popular family attraction.*

   Though Disneyland is a popular family attraction, _____

   _____

Now use your own conjunctions to complete these sentences.

1. _____ *the playground was closed, the repairmen fixed the swings.*

2. _____ *Grandma took my brother to the shops, I rang my friend, John.*

3. _____ *the weather improves dramatically, we will not be going camping.*

4. _____ *our computer is repaired, we will have to borrow Tim's.*

The following sentences are written in the first person. Rewrite them so they are in the third person.

1. *I spilt lemonade on my skirt, although it didn't stain it.*

   _____

2. *Once the roadworks are finished, we will ride our bikes to school.*

   _____

3. *I am two years older than my brother.*

   _____

Name

Commas

Add commas to the sentences below.

1. I caught the bus which was ten minutes late so that I could buy some new shoes.
2. Although it was raining we went outside to pick up litter from the playground.
3. We all sang songs to cheer ourselves up despite the terrific noise of the explosions.
4. On our class visit to the Sea Life Centre last week we saw amongst other things dolphins performing some amazing tricks.
5. Our family holiday which was the first we had taken abroad was spoilt by the poor weather.
6. I enjoy spending my pocket money on books whereas my sister prefers spending hers on CDs.

Brackets and dashes

Rewrite these sentences by adding brackets or dashes .

1. ARP Air Raid Precautions committees were set up by the government.

   _____

2. Simret the goalie won the Player of the Year Award at school.

   _____

3. The boy was sitting on the floor stunned.

   _____

4. I peered into the tattered old box and there in the corner was a gold nugget!

   _____

5. Tom Margaret's cousin was very brave.

   _____

Helpful hints for writing an impersonal recount

✦ Remember you are writing to give the reader important information. Select important events or incidents to include in your recount. Try to write about these in the order that they happened.

✦ The opening paragraph should give the reader information about what or who the recount is about. It should answer the questions: 'who', 'what', 'when' and 'where'. This paragraph sets the scene for the reader.

✦ Your recount should be written in the past tense.

The German air force <u>began</u> to bomb London and other large British cities in September 1942.

There <u>was</u> barely enough room for everyone, and the conditions in the shelter <u>were</u> not very pleasant.

✦ Write in the third person.

The thing <u>he</u> will remember most was the noise coming from above ground – it was deafening and very frightening.

<u>They</u> never knew if it was <u>their</u> street, or even <u>their</u> house, that had been hit.

✦ Group sentences about the same subject or idea into paragraphs.

✦ Remember that the reader wasn't there so you need to add details and description to bring the incidents alive for them. But do not write about every single minor detail.

✦ You can add interest to your recount by including illustrations or diagrams. Remember to include a caption for each one.

An Anderson shelter

✦ Your last paragraph should be a closing statement that is a comment about the events. It may remind the reader why they are so important to you or to others.

Impersonal recount
Scaffold 1

You are going to write a recount about the daily life of a person in the past.
To help you plan your account, use the framework below.
Choose one option from each stage as appropriate.

Stage One

Choose one of the following:

a) A servant in a large Victorian house.

b) A child evacuee leaving London during the Second World War to go and live in a house in the country.

c) A wealthy Roman living in Britain.

Research your subject by using a range of sources, such as books, the Internet, CD-Roms and so on.

Stage Two

Use your opening paragraph to set the scene and provide some basic information.

Write briefly about such things as:

a) Who the person is.

b) How old he/she was at the time.

c) The year or time period.

d) Where he/she lived.

Don't go into too much detail yet.

Stage Three

Write some background information about where the person lived.

Now write in more detail about:

a) The house the person lived in. How big was it? How many rooms? What furniture did it have?

b) Who else lived in the house. Who did the person live with? What were their names? What did they do?

c) The neighbourhood. Who else lived nearby? What were the other houses like in the street?

Stage Four

Write some information about the person's daily life.

a) Describe some of the daily duties the person had to perform. Select two or three to write about. Use a separate paragraph for each one.

b) Describe any hobbies/interests the person had. What did they do on a day off/in their spare time?

c) Describe any visits/holidays the person had. Did they go to the seaside? What sorts of things did they do/see?

Stage Five

Write about a particular event in the person's life.

Write about something important that happened to this person or the person's family.

a) Write about a sad event. Why was it so sad for the person? Who helped the person get over this sadness? What happened in the end?

b) Write about a very happy event that happened to this person. Why was the event so good? How did the person react? What happened next?

c) Write about an exciting event – something that the person was planning for a long, long time. Describe the event itself and what part the person had in it. Who else was there? What happened in the end?

Stage Six

Use your final paragraph to conclude your account.

Write briefly about things such as:

a) How the events affected/changed the person.

b) What happened to the person in the end.

c) Did the events impact on other people's lives?

Impersonal recount
Vocabulary bank 1

allowed	exhausted	school
angry	experience	scullery
attacked	frightened	servant
bombs	funny	soldier
chores	furniture	terrible
difficult	hobbies	tired
duties	housework	visit
evacuate	legion	war
evacuee	lonely	wealthy
every day	neighbours	wonderful
everyone	parents	worried
exciting	scary	

My own words

Impersonal recount
Scaffold 2

You are going to write a recount of an historical event.
To help you plan your account, use the framework below.
Choose one option from each stage as appropriate.

Stage One

Choose one of the following:

a) The sinking of 'Titanic'.

b) The coronation of Queen Elizabeth II.

c) The London blitz of the Second World War.

Research your subject by using a range of sources, such as books, the Internet and CD-Roms.

Stage Two

Use your opening paragraph to set the scene and provide some basic information.

Write briefly about such things as:

a) The date(s) the event took place.

b) Where the event happened.

c) Who was involved.

d) What happened.

Don't go into too much detail yet.

Stage Three

Write some background information about things that happened before the event.

Now write in more detail about:

a) The events that occurred in the months before the event. Why were these earlier events so important?

b) The most important people involved in preparing for the event.

c) The preparations that took place in order for the event to happen.

Stage Four

Write some background information about things that happened during the event.

Write in more detail about:

a) The most important people involved in the event. What did they do? What were their roles? How did they behave? What did they look like/how did they dress?

b) The scene where the event took place. What was so special about it? Describe what it was like there.

c) The most frightening/interesting things that took place. How did people react? What sorts of things did they do?

Stage Five

Write some background information about things that happened after the event.

Write in more detail about:

a) How the event ended. What happened?

b) How the event changed people's lives.

c) What was so different about this event from anything else that had happened before.

Stage Six

Use your final paragraph to conclude your account.

Write briefly about things such as:

a) Why the event is still remembered today.

b) What people learned after experiencing the event.

c) How the event influenced future events.

HOW SHALL I CONCLUDE THE ACCOUNT?

Impersonal recount
Vocabulary bank 2

air raid shelter
ambulance
anticipation
blitz
bombing
broadcast
bunting
celebration
ceremony
chaos
crater
crew
crowd
crown
deafening
departure
despair
desperation

destruction
excitement
farewells
fear
fire brigade
frightening
hospital
iceberg
injured
jubilation
life-raft
liner
luxurious
majesty
orb
pageant
panic
patriotic

population
procession
rapid
relief
rescue
sacrifice
sceptre
soldier
steward
survivors
terrified
throng
torrent
tragedy
tragic
unsinkable

My own words

A personal letter

18 Kings Road
Fenton-on-Sea
FR2 5FT

18th August

Dear Simone,

I know it's only been a short while since I last wrote to you, but you'll never guess what happened to me last week. I saved a dolphin's life!

I know that sounds incredible, but honestly it's true. It all started last Sunday morning. The weather was fantastic – red-hot and perfect blue skies (for a change!) Mum and Dad were busy in the garden and I was bored, so I decided to go for a walk along the cliffs. You know, the ones where we went last time you stayed with us.

I'd been walking for a while when I stopped at our secret spot – you remember, the group of boulders past the lighthouse – to sit and admire the view. I had only been there for a few minutes when I noticed a dark shape that seemed to be moving across the sea. I watched it carefully as it slid across the bay. I was intrigued by it; you know what a nosy creature I am. It wasn't a boat and I was sure it wasn't anyone swimming.

I decided to get a better look at it, so I walked back to the lighthouse where there's one of those telescopes you put twenty pence in. It took me two goes before I could focus on the mysterious black shape I had seen earlier. I couldn't believe my eyes when I finally got it in my sights. It was a dolphin! A beautiful, shiny and sleek dolphin here in boring Fenton-On-Sea, and I was looking right at it. I don't know if it was my imagination, but I'm sure it knew it was being watched because right at that moment it leapt clear of the water and seemed to sail through the air. Well you can imagine the excitement I felt. I'd never seen a dolphin in the flesh before, and here one was performing just for me. Just then the money ran out and the telescope went black so I ran down to the beach to get a closer look.

When I reached the beach I was surprised to find it deserted, seeing as it was such a beautiful day. Usually you can't move it's so crowded. I paddled out into the water to get even closer to this wonderful creature that had come to visit our shores. I could see it really clearly now as it put on a wonderful acrobatic display just for me. This must have lasted for about ten minutes before it dived into the waves and disappeared. I waited for about half an hour hoping it would reappear but it didn't; so I rushed back home to tell Mum and Dad.

They didn't believe me at first. Dad said that it couldn't have been a dolphin as they never came this close to shore. Mum thought it might have been a trick of the light on the surface of the water. I felt a bit peeved that they didn't believe me but I insisted that I had seen what I had seen. Eventually they reluctantly accepted what I had told them, but really I think they just wanted to humour me.

Later that afternoon, I went back to see if it was still there but there was no sign of it. By then the beach was packed with families enjoying the sun, so I asked a few people if they had seen a dolphin swimming in the bay, but no one had. I went home wondering if I would ever see it again.

I didn't have to wait long. The very next morning I got up really early (six o'clock!) and went back to the cliffs. Sure enough the dolphin had returned, but it wasn't swimming around like it had the day before. It was lying on the beach. Now I don't know much about the behaviour of dolphins but I was sure that they didn't usually climb onto the sand and sunbathe!

I ran as fast I could down to the beach. It was lying on its side close to the water's edge stranded high and dry. I approached it carefully as I didn't want to frighten it. It was breathing heavily as if it was trying to catch its breath. Its skin was no longer sleek and shiny but dull and dry. I knew dolphins couldn't survive for long out of water and I didn't know how long it had been lying there already. I looked around to find something that would hold water. Luckily I found a sandcastle bucket someone had left on the sand. I filled it with water and poured it all over the dolphin. I'm sure it looked at me and tried to smile. Unfortunately the bucket wasn't very big so I had to keep rushing back and forth desperately trying to keep it wet.

I knew it was too big for me to move on my own. I needed help, and fast. I ran back along the beach to the beach office where the lifeguards worked. There was no one about, it was still too early. I began to panic wondering what to do. Then I remembered the Sea Life Centre at Wixton, which is about twenty miles away. I ran to the phone-box and rang them. A lovely lady answered the phone and, after I had told her what had happened, told me not to worry – they would send a team immediately. She told me to go back to the dolphin and carry on pouring water over it until they arrived.

When I got back the dolphin was all dry again and tiny tears seemed to be slowly oozing from its eyes. I swear it was crying. After about ten minutes I was exhausted with all the effort of running backwards and forward with buckets of water. Fortunately for me, and the dolphin, a man walking along the prom saw what was happening and came over. He asked me if there was anything he could do to help and how long I had been there. He was very kind and calm and took over with the bucket to give me a rest. We carried on for what seemed like ages before we heard the sound of a vehicle driving quickly along the beach. It was the Sea Life people arriving. Three men and a woman got out and introduced themselves. The woman, whose name was Amanda, was the person I had spoken to on the phone earlier.

They quickly examined the poor creature that was becoming more distressed by the minute. They were very calm and certainly seemed to know what they were doing. They began to dig away the soft sand underneath it so that they could slide a canvas sling under its body. When they had done this they attached the sling to a rope and then attached the rope to the front of the vehicle. Slowly they began to drag the dolphin towards the water. The vehicle actually drove into the sea until the water was almost over the top of the wheels. As soon as the water began to lap around the dolphin it seemed to get stronger and began to move around. When it was in deep enough water they carefully unhooked the sling and moved quietly away. For a few moments the dolphin lay there still again, and then with one quick flick of its tail it swam out of the sling and into the water. It dived down so it was completely submerged and then reappeared a few yards away. It turned towards us and made a series of high pitched squeaks before diving again and headed out to the open sea. I like to think it was saying 'thank you'.

We all cheered as it swam away. Amanda thanked me for all I had done and told me that I could have free tickets to the Sea Life Centre any time I wanted. Just then a reporter and photographer appeared and interviewed me and took my picture for the local paper. Heaven knows how they got to hear about it so quickly.

When I got home Mum told me off for being so long, but soon repented when I told what had happened. Dad said, 'You're a hero, that's what you are!' Ever since he has been calling me David Attenborough! When the paper came out they cut the article out and framed it and it's now hanging on the kitchen wall. We haven't been to the Sea Life Centre yet but when we do I will write again and tell you all about it.

So there you are, the story of how I saved a dolphin. Next time you come and stay with us maybe we can go the Sea Life Centre or, who knows, see a dolphin in the bay. And hopefully this time it won't get itself stuck on the beach. I don't think I could go through all the drama again.

Look forward to seeing you again,

Love

Serena

Understanding the grammar and punctuation

Nouns

A noun is a word that refers to somebody, something or a place.

mother, father, skin, water, beach, cliff, dolphin

A noun phrase is a group of words that acts in the same way as a noun in a sentence.

The dark, sleek shape moved across the bay.

Nouns must agree with the verb in a sentence.

The dolphin were lying on the beach.

is not correct.

It should be:

The dolphin was lying on the beach.

Types of nouns

Proper nouns are the names of particular places, people or things. They always begin with a capital letter.

Simone, Kings Road, England, January

Common nouns name things.

mother, water, dolphin, cliff

Collective nouns are the names of groups of things.

class, family, herd, swarm

Direct and indirect speech

There are two ways of reporting what someone has said – directly and indirectly.

Direct speech is when the writer quotes the actual words spoken by someone.

'Don't worry, we will send help immediately,' the lady said.

Indirect speech is when the writer reports what was said but without actually using all the words spoken. It summarises what was said.

The lady told me not to worry, they would send help immediately.

Name

Nouns

Read these sentences and underline the nouns and noun phrases.

1. *There wasn't a cloud in the sky when I got out of bed this morning.*
2. *The whole school met in the hall for a special assembly.*
3. *The fastest athletes were selected for the forthcoming championship.*
4. *'Which of these creatures are mammals?' the teacher asked.*
5. *My sister is a very talented musician. She can play the organ, cello and several percussion instruments.*

In the box below are some nouns. Some are common nouns, some proper nouns and some collective nouns. Rearrange them into three groups. Remember all proper nouns begin with a capital letter.

desk sunlight tuesday thought birmingham brood july pavement
constellation amanda hospital radiator camp asia pride chapters
president forest amazon gaggle

common nouns	proper nouns	collective nouns

Rewrite these sentences so that the noun and verb agree.

1. *The children was playing on the beach.*

   _____

2. *The dolphin are very sick.*

   _____

3. *The shells is very beautiful.*

   _____

Direct and indirect speech

The sentences below are written using direct speech. Rewrite them using indirect speech. The first one has been done for you.

1. The tour guide said, 'Today's trip is to the ancient castle and leaves at nine o'clock and returns at five.'
    The tour guide told us that the trip today was to the ancient castle and that we leave at nine o'clock and return at five.

2. Ryan shouted, 'Last one in the sea buys the ice creams!'
    _____

3. It was while we were walking to school that Simon asked, 'Shall we go the swimming baths after school?'
    _____
    _____

4. 'Never play on or near the railway lines,' the policeman told the class.
    _____

The sentences below are written using indirect speech. Rewrite them using direct speech. Make sure you use the correct punctuation in each one.

1. The travel agent asked me where I would like to go on holiday and how many tickets I would need.
    _____
    _____

2. Our swimming coach told us that we had to train at least three times a week if we wanted to get into the team.
    _____
    _____

3. The dog's owner was very angry and shouted that we should keep our dog on a lead when we were walking it in the park.
    _____
    _____

4. The nurse said that my little brother had been very brave.
    _____

Helpful hints for writing a personal letter

✦ Think carefully about what you want to tell the person you are writing to before you begin the letter.

✦ Put your own address and the date in the top right-hand corner of the page.

✦ On the next line against the left-hand margin write 'Dear' followed by the person's name.

✦ Write as if you are talking to your friend. A personal letter can be chatty and friendly.

> *I know it's only been a short while since I last wrote to you, but you'll never guess what happened to me last week.*

✦ Include personal opinions and information.

> *The weather was fantastic... (for a change!)*

✦ Try to write about things that will make the reader laugh and enjoy reading the letter.

> *Now I don't know much about the behaviour of dolphins but I was sure that they didn't usually climb onto the sand and sun bathe!*

✦ You can include reminders about things you have done in the past with the reader of your letter.

> *You know, the ones where we went last time you stayed with us.*

✦ Try to make your letter interesting for the reader by not writing about ordinary, everyday things like what you had for lunch or what you watched on television. Try to write about something that you think they will enjoy reading about.

✦ You can use slang words in personal letters.

> *cool (good), kid (child), cop (policeman), plonker (stupid person)*

But remember you should not use the same kind of language writing to your grandmother as you might to your best friend! (Granny might not understand you!)

✦ Your last paragraph can be used to sum up what you have written in the letter. Finish off with something warm and friendly like 'give my love to' or 'don't forget to write back'.

✦ Sign off with 'Love' for a family member or close friend or 'Best wishes' or 'Kind regards' for others. Then sign your name. You only need to write your first name because the reader knows who you are.

✦ If you have forgotten to put something in the letter, you can add a P.S. at the end. But keep this short.

> *P.S. Don't forget we are going to the gym next week.*

Personal letter
Scaffold 1

You are going to write a personal account of something that happened to you. You will write this account in the form of a letter to a friend/ family member.

Your style will be informal and should include your own opinions and comments on the events about which you are writing.

Choose one option from each stage.

Stage One

Decide to whom you are writing.

a) A friend who is the same age as you.

b) Your aunty who lives in Australia.

c) Your grandfather who lives a long way from where you live.

Stage Two

Give the reason for writing.

You are writing in response to their recent letter telling you that he/she is feeling fed up at the moment. You decide to write a letter that will cheer him/her up.

You decide to write about:

a) A recent holiday or day out.

b) Your best or worst day at school.

c) A recent birthday or special event such as Christmas.

Stage Three

Set the scene for what you are writing about.

Write about how the day began. Try to draw the reader into the mood of the day. Remember to use a friendly, chatty style.

Tell them about:

a) Something strange or funny that happened when you woke up.

b) Something unusual that happened as you were eating breakfast.

c) How the family pet caused you lots of bother before the day had even started.

Stage Four

Now write about the main events or incidents of the day.

Write these in the order they happened. Include something funny or horrible that happened to you. Remember, you are writing to cheer up the person you are writing to so try to make the day / event sound interesting.

Explain why the day was so special / disastrous.

a) You received a surprise gift / treat that absolutely amazed you.

b) An unexpected guest / person turned up.

c) You created an accident of some kind.

Stage Five

Describe how the day finished.

Explain what happened in the end.

a) Explain why it was the best / worst day of your life.

b) Describe one more funny / horrible event.

c) Explain why you will never forget that day.

Stage Six

Sign off appropriately.

a) Take care and lots of love,

b) Look forward to hearing from you soon,

c) With love from,

Personal letter
Vocabulary bank 1

absolutely
accident
afternoon
amazing
answer, reply
best
breakfast
catastrophe
disaster
everyone
exciting
family
fantastic
frightened

Guess what
   happened?
holiday
How are you?
important
incredible
laughing
morning
nearly
never
recent letter
sorry to hear
special
strange

surprise
terrific
thank you
trouble
unhappy
unusual
very
want
worried
worst
you'll never guess

My own words

Personal letter
Scaffold 2

You are going to write a personal account of something that happened to you.
You will write this account in the form of a letter to a friend/family member.
Your style will be informal and should include your own opinions and comments on the events about which you are writing.
Choose one option from each stage.

Stage One

Decide to whom you are writing.

a) A friend who is the same age as you who recently moved to another county.

b) Your uncle who lives in Spain and works in a hotel there.

c) Your grandmother who lives a long way away but often visits you.

Stage Two

Give the reason for writing.

You are writing to invite the person to stay for a week in order to help prepare a surprise birthday party for your sister/brother who is turning 18.

a) You want him/her to help you make the party decorations.

b) You want him/her to help you make your present for your sister/brother (Describe what it is.).

c) Your parents want you to be occupied with someone else while they do all the preparations.

Stage Three

Explain what else he/she will be doing during their visit.

Try and tempt your guest to agree to stay by telling them about other things you would like to do with them during their stay:

a) going to the pictures to see his/her favourite film;

b) going on a picnic;

c) visiting his/her favourite museum/theme park.

Stage Four

Tell your invited guest about what you have been doing lately.

Write about the main events or incidents of the past two or three weeks that you think will interest them.

a) Tell them about something funny that happened to you.

b) Tell them about a place you went to visit.

c) Tell them about something your pet(s) did that was very unusual.

Add interest to your recount by not just telling what happened but by describing the most significant events in some detail.

- Use imaginative language.

- Avoid including unimportant details.

- Include your own comments on the events. Describe how you were feeling at the time. Were you amused, excited or surprised by the things that happened?

Stage Five

Sum up the letter.

End your letter by writing a concluding paragraph which summarises the whole experience or brings your recount to a natural finish.

Use phrases like:

a) So as you can see it's been …

b) I hope you have enjoyed hearing about …

c) Finally…

d) After all this excitement I'm looking forward to…

e) So who knows what will happen next.

Sign off your letter in a friendly informal style.

Love from
(your name)

Personal letter
Vocabulary bank 2

absolutely
annoyed
answer, reply
anxious
appreciate
banquet
beautiful
birthday
brilliant
celebrate
celebrations
colourful
conclusion
decorations

dessert
disco
entertainment
exciting
fantastic
favourite
grateful
guest
happened
hundred
invitation
lately
magnificent
marvellous

neighbours
occasion
organise
parcels
party
please
preparations
sensational
spectacular
surprise
thank you
unusual

My own words

How to keep fish

The following instructions will teach you how to:

1. set up an indoor fish tank to keep your fish in;
2. safely introduce your fish to the tank;
3. correctly feed your fish;
4. care for your fish tank.

SETTING UP YOUR FISH TANK

You need the following materials:

✦ one large, glass fish tank;
✦ one electric water pump and filter;
✦ landscaping materials such as pea-gravel, rocks and stones;
✦ one bottle of tap water conditioner;
✦ one water thermometer;
✦ several underwater plants.

What to do

1. Clean your new tank, but do not use any detergents, then rinse out the tank with fresh water.
2. Wash the landscaping materials.
3. Place about seven centimetres of gravel on the base of the tank. Ensure the gravel slopes from the back of the tank towards the front.
4. Add your landscaping materials, such as rocks and stones.
5. Attach the filter and pump to the tank. **Ask an adult to connect the electric cables.**
6. Fix the thermometer to the front of the tank.
7. Prepare the tap water by adding water conditioner – follow the instructions on the bottle.
8. Fill your tank with the prepared water.
9. Wash your underwater plants.
10. Place the plants in the tank, putting the tallest ones at the back.
11. Place the lid on the tank.
12. Turn on the pump and filter.
13. Let the tank stand for at least a week before buying your fish. Only buy a small number of fish at first and gradually add to them over several weeks.

INTRODUCING YOUR FISH INTO THE TANK

You need the following materials:

+ your new fish;
+ one water thermometer;
+ one plastic jug;
+ one small net.

You should not put your fish straight into your new tank because the water in the bag that your new fish are in will be at a different temperature to the water in your tank. If you do your fish may become unwell and die.

Follow these steps to ensure your fish are healthy and happy in their new home.

What to do

1. Turn off the pump and filter.
2. Lift off the lid.
3. Float the bag of fish in your tank for at least 20 minutes so that the temperature of the water in the bag becomes the same as the water in the tank.
4. Check the temperature of the water in the bag and in the tank. **Ensure that they are equal before proceeding to step five.**
5. Scoop out some water from the tank using a plastic jug then pour it gently into the open bag of fish.
6. After five minutes add some more water by repeating step five. This will allow the fish to adjust to their new water.
7. Place your small net inside the bag and lift out the fish one at a time and put them straight into the tank.
8. Put the lid back on the tank.
9. Switch on the pump and filter.

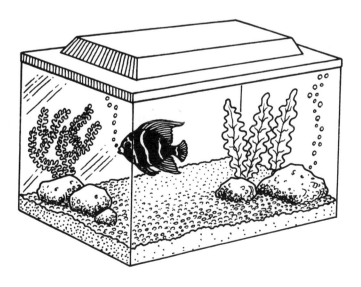

FEEDING YOUR FISH

You need the following materials:

- ✦ complete flake food for fish;
- ✦ frozen, freeze-dried or fresh live food.

What to do

1. Feed your fish *once a day* with complete flake food.
   - Give them only a *small* pinch.
   - Sprinkle the crushed flakes over the surface of the water.
2. Feed your fish *once a week* with frozen, freeze-dried or fresh live food instead of flakes.

CARING FOR YOUR FISH TANK

It is important to care for your tank so that your fish and plants stay healthy.

You need the following materials:

- ✦ water thermometer;
- ✦ one nitrate testing kit;
- ✦ one magnetic glass scraper;
- ✦ one scouring pad;
- ✦ one scrubbing brush;
- ✦ one sponge.

What to do

Every day

1. Check the water filter is working.
2. Check the water temperature morning and night.
3. Carry out a nitrate test for the first two weeks by following the manufacturer's instructions.

Every two weeks

1. Scrape the algae off the inside of the tank using the magnetic scraper.
2. Change the water filter.
3. Change one tenth of the tank water, remembering to prepare the new water with conditioner (see step 7 of 'Setting Up Your New Tank').
4. Clean the gravel.
5. Wipe the lid of the tank.

YOU ARE NOW READY TO KEEP AND ENJOY HEALTHY FISH!

Understanding the grammar and punctuation

Technical vocabulary
These are the special words the writer needs to use when writing instructions.

complete _flake food_

magnetic _scraper_

nitrate testing kit

Verb tenses
The tense of a verb tells you when the action is taking place.

There are three main tenses:

Present: tells you what is happening now;

Past: tells you what has happened previously – in the past;

Future: tells you what is still to happen in the future.

Instructions are written in the present tense.

It is important to care for your tank so that your fish and plants stay healthy.

Connectives
Connectives are words or phrases that link clauses and sentences.
Connectives used in instructions are often time related.

then rinse out the tank

after five minutes add some more water

Imperative verbs
Verbs used as commands are called imperative.

Place the lid on the tank.

Feed your fish every morning and night.

Check the water filter is working.

Colon
A colon looks like this :

It is used to introduce a list.

You need the following materials:
- _one large, glass fish tank;_
- _one electric water pump and filter;_
- _landscaping materials such as pea-gravel, rocks and stones;_
- _one bottle of tap water conditioner;_
- _one water thermometer;_
- _several underwater plants._

Imperative verbs and sentences

Imperative verbs are used as commands or instructions. In an imperative sentence the verb usually comes at the start of the sentence. The sentences are often short so that the command or instruction is clear.

Below is some text that describes Fiona's journey from home to school. Rewrite them as simple instructions. Remember to number each instruction and start each sentence with a strong verb. For example: Turn right at the library.

When you get to the end of the garden path turn left and walk along the road until you come to the end of the road. When you get to the end of the road cross the road and carry on until you get to the library. When you get to the library, turn right along Hope Street. When you reach Fellows Lane turn left into it. Carry on walking along Fellows Lane until you come to the petrol station. Cross the road there and turn left. Carry on walking for about a hundred metres and the school is on your left.

_____

_____

_____

_____

_____

_____

_____

_____

_____

On the back of this sheet, write imperative sentences using the verbs below. Start each sentence with the verb. One has been done for you.

hold   wash   check   measure   wipe   find   draw   call   follow   take

Wash your hands before eating.

Using colons to introduce a list

A colon looks like this :
It is used to introduce a list.

Below is a recipe for making scrambled eggs on toast. It is written in prose, so it is not easy for the reader to identify what utensils and ingredients are needed.

Crack three or four eggs into a bowl. Measure out 100 millilitres of milk and stir the eggs and milk together. Weigh out 50 grams of butter and put it into a small saucepan and gently melt the butter on the cooker. While the butter is melting put the bread into the toaster. When the butter is melted add the egg and milk mixture and stir until the mixture becomes solid. Remove the saucepan from the cooker and butter the toast. Spoon the scrambled eggs onto the buttered toast.

Write a set of instructions for making the scrambled eggs.
1. Make sure you start with a list of ingredients introduced by a colon.
2. Then write a list of utensils introduced by a colon.
3. Finally, write out a list of commands telling the reader what to do at each stage.

_____

_____

_____

_____

_____

_____

_____

_____

_____

_____

_____

_____

Helpful hints for writing instructions

Organising the text

✦ A set of instructions has to be in the correct order so plan your instructions carefully.

✦ Research your subject thoroughly by reading as much as you can. Use books, encyclopaedias, pamphlets, CD-Roms and the Internet.

✦ Collect information and make notes before writing the instructions.

✦ Work out the exact order of tasks so they are logical, easy to follow and in the correct order. Make it clear what the reader has to do first, second and so on until the task is completed successfully.

✦ Choose a title that makes it very clear what the instructions will enable the reader to do.

   How to Keep Fish

✦ At the beginning of your text write the specific goal of the instructions.

   These following instructions will teach you how to...

✦ Follow this by writing a series of steps the reader has to follow. Make sure they are detailed enough so that the reader can follow them accurately and easily.

✦ Make sure the instructions tell the reader *how*, *where* and *when* each step is to be carried out

   Prepare the water by adding water conditioner.

Place your small net inside the bag...

After five minutes add some more water...

✦ Finish by referring back to the specific goal of the instructions.

   You are now ready to keep and enjoy healthy fish!

Layout

✦ Make sure you include the following sections:

   • the specific goal to be achieved;

   • a list of the materials needed and their quantity;

   • a set of steps to follow.

✦ Write your text in sections and lay it out so these different sections are clear.

✦ Highlight the start of each section by writing a heading in big bold lettering. Or you could layout the text in the form of a table.

✦ Use bullet points and numbers to show the order of the steps.

✦ Use bold print to highlight the headings and important safety issues.

✦ Use illustrations/diagrams to make the instructions even easier to follow.

Instructions
Scaffold 1

You are going to write a set of instructions about keeping a pet.
To help plan your text use the framework below.
Choose one option from each stage.

Stage One

Decide which pet you are going to write care instructions for.

a) A hamster.

b) A guinea-pig.

c) A dog.

d) A pet of your own choice.

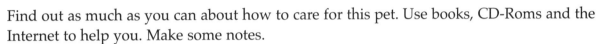

Find out as much as you can about how to care for this pet. Use books, CD-Roms and the Internet to help you. Make some notes.

Stage Two

Write a list of the equipment/items needed to care for the pet.

Set it out in one of the following ways:

a) as a numbered list;

b) inside a box;

c) as a bullet point list.

Put a heading at the top in bold.

Stage Three

Write a paragraph explaining what the instructions are about.

Choose one of these beginnings.

a) These instructions will tell you how to care for a _____ (type of pet).

b) Keeping a _____ (type of pet) can be great fun. These instructions will help you to care for it correctly.

c) If you would like to know how to care properly for _____ (type of pet) please follow these instructions.

Then write a list of things an owner should consider when buying this type of pet.

Stage Four

Put a heading: Bedding/housing

Write a set of instructions on how to prepare the correct bedding/housing for this type of pet. Make sure you include information about pet safety and hygiene.

Think about what the pet should be kept in:
✦ How large will it need to be?
✦ What should it be made from?
✦ What floor covering is necessary? How often should it be changed?
✦ What can be used to create hiding/sleeping places?
✦ What things can be put inside for the pet to play with?
✦ Where should it be kept?

Remember to write each step as an imperative sentence with the verb at the beginning of each sentence. Try to be as detailed as possible and use appropriate technical language. Include labelled diagrams.

Stage Five

Put a heading: Feeding

Write a set of instructions on how to feed this type of pet.

Include information about the following:
a) the types of food/drink the pet should have;
b) how often the pet should be fed;
c) the kind of food containers that should be used. How often they should be cleaned;
d) where to buy the food;
e) how to store the food.

Stage Six

Write a short conclusion to round off your instructions.

Choose from the following:

a) If you follow these instructions your pet will...

b) These instructions will help ensure that your pet...

c) Finally, ...

Instructions
Vocabulary bank 1

adequate
appropriate
aquarium
bedding
blanket
bowl
brush
cage
carefully
chew
collar
comb
comfortable
daily

diet
disinfectant
draught
every
exercise
fortnight
grooming
healthy
hutch
lead
night
odour
patience
safety

shredded newspaper
space
special
straw
strong
sufficient
teething
temperature
training
ventilation
veterinary surgeon
water
waterproof
weekly

My own words

Instructions
Scaffold 2

You are going to write a set of instructions on how to make something.
To help plan your instructions, use the framework below.
Choose one option from each stage, or use your own ideas.

Stage One

Decide what the instructions are going to be about.

a) How to make a model car.

b) How to make a papier-mâché mask.

c) How to make a cake or some biscuits.

Find out as much as you can about your chosen subject and make notes on what you learn.

Stage Two

Write a list of the equipment/ingredients/materials needed to make the item.

Set it out in the following way:

a) as a numbered list;

b) inside a box;

c) as a bullet point list.

Put a heading at the top in bold.

Stage Three

Write a paragraph explaining what the instructions are about.

Choose one of these beginnings.

a) These instructions will tell you how to make a _____

b) Follow these instructions to make a _____

c) In order to make a perfect _____

Get the reader interested by making it seem an enjoyable thing to do!

Stage Four

Write the heading: What to do

Write down step-by-step instructions on how to make the item.

✦ Decide what the reader needs to do first, second and so on.

✦ Make sure each step is detailed enough for them to carry it out correctly.

✦ Decide if each step needs an illustration or if only selected ones require this additional information.

Remember to write each step as an imperative sentence with the verb at the beginning of each sentence. For example,

Mix the water and paste.

Glue the four corner pieces together using wood glue and cardboard fixing plates.

Try to be as detailed as possible and use appropriate technical language.

Stage Five

Write the heading: Important things to remember.

Write a list of important hints and tips for the reader. Such as:
a) safety/hygiene issues that need to be considered;
b) how to use equipment correctly;
c) how to avoid certain mistakes.

Decide how to present your list:
a) numbered points;
b) bullet points;
c) lettering.

Stage Six

Write a short conclusion to round off your instructions.

Choose from the following.

a) Now that you have made the_____, you can enjoy…

b) Your_____is now ready to use/eat. The best way to enjoy it is…

c) You should have now successfully made your_____. Remember…

Instructions
Vocabulary bank 2

adhesive	decorate	length
adjacent	diagram	measure
allow	diameter	middle
apparatus	dowel	opposite
approximate	entire	papier-mâché
arrange	essential	parallel
assemble	fasten	paste
attach	fibre	pinch
bake, baking	flavour	quantity
baste	fold	ruler
beat	fresh	scissors
boil	front	score
bowl	gather	screwdriver
break	glue	sculpture
carve	half	smooth
centimetre	healthy	tasty
circumference	ingredient	temperature
container	join, joint	thread
craft-knife	kilogram	varnish
cross section	kitchen	width

My own words

Antarctica – An Ice Desert

Antarctica is the highest, coldest and windiest continent on Earth. It is also a desert – an ice desert. It is remote, hostile and uninhabited like all the great deserts. It is an extraordinary area and a place of extremes and is of great interest to scientists. Antarctica is the fifth largest continent and makes up approximately ten per cent of the world's land mass. In the summer months it covers an area of approximately 14.2 million square miles, which is about one and a half

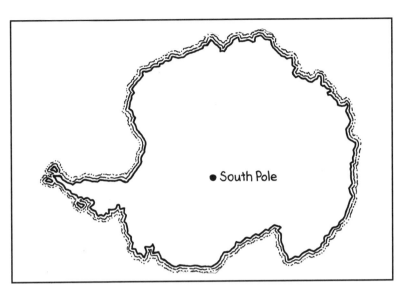

A map of Antarctica

times the size of Europe and 58 times larger than the United Kingdom. However during the winter months it appears to double in size, due to ice sheets spreading out as the surrounding ocean freezes over. It is different from the Arctic because the Antarctic is a land mass covered in a thick ice sheet and the Arctic is a mass of ice that floats on the water of the Arctic Ocean.

Climate and weather

The climate of Antarctica is extreme. It has six months of continuous daylight during the summer and six months of continuous darkness during the winter. In every area the temperatures are cold. Along the low lying coasts the average temperature is around –12°C; higher up on the ice-cap the average is –20°C; and at the highest points up in the mountains it is –60°C. Even in the summer months the temperatures are low. There are two main reasons for this. Firstly, the Sun does not climb very high above the horizon and the rays are spread over

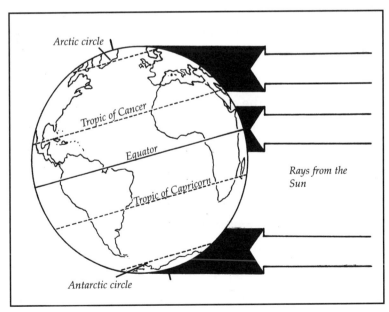

Temperatures at the poles are always lower than at the Equator. The Sun's rays are more spread out and they have further to travel, so they lose more of their heat.

a wide area which weakens their warming effect. In the tropics the Sun rises much higher in the sky and the rays are concentrated in a small area making the effect more pronounced. Secondly, the ice does not absorb much heat from the Sun because it acts like a mirror and reflects the Sun's rays back into the atmosphere. In areas of the world that are free from ice and snow, between 15 and 30 per cent of the Sun's radiation is reflected back into the atmosphere, compared to about 80 per cent reflected back in Antarctica.

It is not only the temperatures that are extreme in Antarctica. Tremendous winds blow across the continent. These usually begin in the centre of the continent (which is the coldest area) and flow outwards to the coast, gathering speed as they go. They can reach an incredible 150 kilometres per hour! As they reach the coast they collide with the warmer air coming in from the ocean and create violent blizzards, cloud and fog.

Many people, when they think of a desert, picture a dry hot place, yet Antarctica is a desert! In fact it is the Earth's largest desert and one of its driest. It has less than the equivalent of 50mm of rain a year. The air is too cold to hold much moisture and even when blizzards are raging around the coastal areas the precipitation (the fall of rain, sleet, snow or hail) is only equivalent to around 40cm of rain a year.

Teams of scientists live on Antarctica to study the climate and weather to help them understand the global changes in climate that are being recorded. They do this by studying the weather patterns, using a range of special measuring instruments, and the ice sheets. The ice sheets, which can be as thick as four kilometres, are a valuable source of information about the climate of the past. Within the ice is a record of the climate of the last 500,000 years. The ice sheets become a little thicker each year as fresh snow falls onto the surface. This squashes the layers below into ice. Core samples are taken by
drilling down into the ice. These are then analysed to calculate how old the ice is. Air and particles (minute portions of matter) of dust or pollen can be found embedded in the ice samples and these tell scientists what the climatic conditions were like at the time. From this study it is clear that the climate has changed over the years, and ice from the last 100 years shows an increasing amount of air pollution.

Antarctica's natural resources

Not all of the scientists working in Antarctica are studying the weather. Some are concerned with finding out what resources might be found there. The geology of the area has been mapped for the last 40 years but as yet there is little evidence of the rich supplies of minerals, oil and natural gas that some believe to be present under the ice. Exposed coal seams are to be found in the Transantarctic Mountains but there do not appear to be sufficient reserves to merit the tremendous expense of extracting it through mining, especially in such difficult conditions. Further investigation through drilling and exploratory mines cannot take place at the present time because there is an international ban on mining on the continent until at least 2041.

More readily available resources are to be found in the Antarctic Ocean. Here there is an abundance of sea life such as whales, seals and fish. Seal hunting has been carried out in the area for well over 100 years and by the 1920s the fur seal was almost hunted to extinction because its fur was popular for the manufacture of hats and felt. Other kinds of seal were also hunted, especially the southern elephant seal for its blubber, which was turned into high-quality oil. Today all seal hunting is closely controlled by an international treaty and the numbers of seals have increased significantly.

There are many species of whale to be found in the surrounding oceans of Antarctica. These include the blue whale, southern bottlenose, minke, humpback, sperm and orca whales. These, like the seals, have been hunted by commercial whalers until many of the species were close to extinction. Since the 1920s more than 1.3 million whales have been killed in the Southern Ocean. They were hunted for their blubber which was used to make detergents and lubricants, and their meat which is a popular delicacy in some parts of the world. Nowadays the hunting of whales is either banned or closely controlled.

Whales – an endangered species?

Name	Estimated numbers	Status
southern bottlenose whale	abundant	secure
blue whale	10,000	endangered
humpback whale	5,000	endangered
minke whale	400,00	endangered
sperm whale	200,00	endangered
right whale	3,000	endangered
orca – killer whale	3,000	endangered

Most species of whales have been severely depleted. Their current status is due largely to commercial whaling, which took place during the 19th and 20th centuries. Most have population estimates far below pre-whaling numbers.

There is an abundance of fish resources partly because the whales that used to feed off them have been hunted and killed. Large factory ships sail into the ocean and from them smaller fishing vessels are launched. These catch large quantities of fish and take them back to the factory ships where the fish is processed and frozen whilst the ship is still at sea. When they are full they sail back to their home port and sell their catch.

The future for Antarctica

Antarctica is a unique and valuable environment for us all. There are several international agreements in place that protect it for the foreseeable future. It is agreed that the main activity in Antarctica should be scientific research and that its natural environment should be protected. The research that is carried out is valuable to us all. We are able to learn more about the Earth's natural systems and how human activities across the globe affect them. The information this research provides enables us to identify global problems and this allows us to decide what action can be taken to resolve them.

Its environment is safe for the time being through international agreements but should valuable resources such as oil and gas be found there will be considerable commercial pressure to extract them. This would undoubtedly result in the environment being damaged to some degree and may mean the end of the Earth's last unspoilt wilderness. Some people are in favour of making Antarctica a World Park where mining and military activities would be prohibited; others believe that we need these resources more than we need to protect Antarctica.

Antarctica is not owned or controlled by any single country so, when the current treaties expire later this century, there will have to be a new international agreement concerning its future. By then the scientists will have discovered even more about this remarkable continent and careful consideration will need to be made about the long-term future of this extraordinary place.

A typical Antarctic landscape scene.

Understanding the grammar and punctuation

Verb tenses

The tense of a verb tells you when the action is taking place.

There are three main tenses:

Present tense – tells you what is happening now.

Antarctica is the highest, coldest and windiest continent on earth.

Past tense – tells you what has already happened.

...the climate <u>has changed</u>.

Future tense – tells you what will happen in the future.

There <u>will be</u> considerable commercial pressure...

Verbs and nouns

A verb must agree with the noun or pronoun in a sentence.

If the noun is plural, then the verb should be plural also.

It is not only the temperatures that <u>is</u> extreme in Antarctica.

The sentence should be written like this:

It is not only the temperatures that <u>are</u> extreme in Antarctica.

Paragraphs

A paragraph is a collection of sentences about the same idea or subject.

✦ Paragraphs can be of different lengths.

✦ The opening sentence of each paragraph often tells the reader what the paragraph is about.

There are many species of whale to be found in the surrounding oceans of Antarctica.

✦ The rest of the paragraph then goes on to list them and tell the reader something about them.

Teams of scientists live on Antarctica to study the climate to help them understand the global changes in climate that are being recorded.

✦ The reader knows when a new paragraph begins because it is either separated from the previous one by leaving a space between them; or by indenting the first word.

Verb tenses

Read the following sentences and underline the verbs in them.

1. Most of the world's supply of gold comes from South Africa.
2. The local football team drew the last three games of the season and finished second in the league.
3. The autumn term will start on the third of September.
4. The river burst its banks and caused tremendous damage to the surrounding area.
5. The shop developed our holiday photographs in less than an hour.
6. We are planning a surprise party for my brother later this month.
7. He saw a group of sharks as he dived down to the wreck lying on the seabed.
8. We are studying the local environment as part of our geography work this term.
9. The explorer reached the South Pole in record time despite covering the last few miles in a blizzard.
10. I think this film is the best yet.

Now write the verbs you underlined in the correct boxes below. When you have done that write the other forms of the verb The first one is done for you.

Past tense	**Present tense**	**Future tense**
came	comes	will come

Verb and noun agreement

In the sentences below the verb and noun do not agree. Change them so that they do.

1. Penguins is a species of bird that can not fly.
2. You is the best swimmer in the class.
3. I likes vanilla flavoured icecream the best.
4. My parents doesn't let me walk to the shops on my own.
5. Trains is much faster than cars.
6. My friends is coming round to my house tonight because I is having a party.
7. You was better at maths than I was.

Name

Paragraphs

The sentences below are all about one general subject – penguins.
Cut them out and sort them into groups under the following headings.

General information   Physical features

Breeding colonies   Enemies

Each set of sentences can then be used to form a paragraph. Write an opening sentence for each paragraph that tells what each is about. Then write each paragraph. You do not have to use the exact words or order of words in the sentences. You can rewrite them and rearrange them as you wish.

Penguins have shiny, waterproof feathers that help them keep their skin dry.

They are insulated against the extreme cold by thick layers of blubber.

Penguins breed in large colonies called 'rookeries'.

The natural enemies of the penguin are seals and killer whales.

Penguins' bones are heavy and solid to help them keep submerged.

Young chicks and eggs are vulnerable to attacks by seabirds.

Only four of the seventeen species of penguins breed on the Antarctic land mass.

Penguins build nests of stone and incubate one or two eggs.

Penguins spend 75 per cent of their lives at sea, but breed on land.

Penguins are truly flightless birds.

Adults take turns to incubate the eggs and to feed the chicks when they hatch.

When swimming they retract their heads to make their shape more hydrodynamic.

Healthy adult birds have no predators on land.

Penguins are usually black and white and found in the southern hemisphere.

Helpful hints for writing non-comparative reports

Research

✦ Find out as much as you can about the subject by researching different sources. Try to use a wide range of sources such as:
- reference books;
- text books;
- magazines;
- CD-Roms;
- the Internet;
- interviewing people.

Planning your text and note taking

✦ When doing your research decide what different areas of the topic you will write about and write headings for them.

✦ As you make your notes, write them under the appropriate heading. This will help you organise them. Write them as bullet points.

✦ Now decide how many paragraphs you will need and put them into order. Remember the first one should be a general introduction to the topic; and the last one should be a short summary of all the main points.

✦ Decide where you will place any diagrams or illustrations you wish to include in your report.

✦ Write each paragraph in draft form using your notes to help you. Start each paragraph with an opening sentence that tells the reader what it about.

Editing your text

✦ Check your draft text for spelling or grammatical errors.

✦ Ensure you have used the present tense throughout.

✦ Ensure you have used 'specialist' vocabulary or technical terms where necessary.

✦ Check that all illustrations or diagrams have captions and labels.

Non-comparative reports
Scaffold 1

You are going to write a report about one general subject.
To help plan your writing, use the framework below.
Choose one option from each stage.

Stage One

Select one of the subjects below to write about.

1. Deserts
2. Tropical rainforests
3. Mountains

Research your subject by collecting together as many sources of information as possible.
Use the library, the Internet and CD-Roms to read as much as you can about your chosen subject.

Stage Two

Make notes on some of the following areas of information and use them for a paragraph plan.

a) What is a desert / rainforest / mountain?
b) Where in the world can they be found?
c) What are the common features?
d) What is the climate like?
e) What animal life can be found there?
f) What plant life can be found there?
g) What natural resources can be found and extracted?

Stage Three

Write a short introduction.
Start your introduction with one of the following phrases:

a) Deserts / tropical rainforests / mountains are found... (where in the world?)
b) Deserts / tropical rainforest / mountains can be some of the most inhospitable places on earth. They are...
c) The world's biggest deserts / tropical rainforests / tallest mountains are found in...
d) A desert / tropical rainforest / mountain is...
e) Humans have always been fascinated with deserts / tropical rainforest / mountains. This is because they are so...

Stage Four

Use your notes under each heading to write about different aspects of your subject. Each set of notes will form a separate paragraph.

Start each paragraph with a sentence that informs the reader what it is about.
You can use some or all of the following, or write your own sentences.

a) Deserts are found in most continents of the world.
b) The climate of all deserts is one of scarce rainfall.
c) Despite appearances deserts do provide homes for a range of animals.
d) Even in the driest most barren of deserts plant life can be found.

e) Tropical rainforests are to be found in the tropics which sit either side of the Equator.
f) The climate of rainforests is hot, wet and humid.
g) An abundance of animal life can be found in rainforests.
h) Rainforests have a great diversity of plant life.

i) Mountains are found all over the world but the Earth's tallest are found in the Himalayas.
j) Mountain climates change the higher up you go.
k) A huge variety of different animals live on and around mountains.
l) Mountains have distinct zones where different plants are able to survive.

Stage Five

Draw or print diagrams, maps, illustrations or tables that provide extra information.

Label each one clearly. Write a caption for each one. Decide where they will go in the text.

The map or diagram might show:

a) where in the world deserts/tropical rainforests/mountains are found;
b) rainfall and temperature information;
c) the area/height of specific deserts rainforests/mountains;
d) the resources found in the regions.

Stage Six

Write a short concluding paragraph to summarise the main points from your text. You could use these or write your own:

a) So we can see that deserts are fascinating environments not barren uninteresting places.

b) Rainforests provide a habitat for over half the world's plant and animal species and must be conserved.

c) Mountains are forbidding places that provide a wealth of resources and recreation for people all over the world.

Non-comparative reports
Vocabulary bank 1

absorb	degrees	landscape
annual	drought	medicines
arid	dunes	moisture
average	evergreen	oasis
bare	explore	rainfall
barren	fauna	shade
climate	flora	snow line
climb	habitat	summit
conquer	heat	temperature
conservation	highest	vegetation
creatures	humid	windswept
crevice	intense	world

My own words

Non-comparative reports
Scaffold 2

You are going to write a report about one general subject.
To help plan your writing, use the framework below.
Choose one option from each stage, or use your own ideas.

Stage One

Select one of the subjects below to write about.

1. The fire brigade.
2. The ambulance service.
3. The police.

Research your subject by collecting together as many sources of information as possible.
Use the library, the Internet and CD-Roms to read as much as you can about your chosen subject.

Stage Two

Decide on your paragraph headings and make notes about each area of information.

You could write about:

a) What the service does;

b) What happens when they receive an emergency call;

c) How they are trained;

d) The equipment they use;

e) The different sort of incidents they attend.

Stage Three

Write a short introduction about what the service is and the general work they do.

You could begin with one of the following or write your own opening sentence:

a) The _____ service was founded to…

b) The _____ provides emergency services to assist the local area in times of need. It also…

c) The _____ is one of several emergency services…

Stage Four

Use your notes and headings to write a paragraph about each aspect of the service. Include details and important information.

You might want to write about:

a) **Emergency calls**: How someone makes a 999 call; how the station is contacted; how the fire fighters / ambulance people / police get ready; how they reach the site of the emergency; what they do when they get there.

b) **Training**: who can train; where they are trained; how they are trained; what they are trained to do; how long training takes.

c) **Equipment**: specialist equipment used; uniforms and protective clothing; special tools.

d) **Incidents**: how they respond to accidents / fires / thefts and so on.

Stage Five

Draw some diagrams, illustrations or tables that provide extra information.

Label each one clearly. Write a caption for each one. Decide where they will go in the text.

The diagram or illustration might show:
a) specialist equipment used;

b) a flow diagram of the processes involved in an emergency call;

c) emergency response times in different counties;

d) specialist uniforms / clothing used.

Stage Six

Write a short conclusion which summarises the work of the service. You could begin by using one of the following phrases or write your own:

a) The fire brigade / ambulance / police help many people each year...

b) The bravery and skill of fire-fighters / ambulance workers / police ensure many lives are saved each year...

c) The _____ not only rescue / help / save people they also...

Non-comparative reports
Vocabulary bank 2

apparatus
arrest
assault
assess
baton
blaze
breathing
casualty
chief
courageous
criminals
dangerous
dense
district
emergency

engulfed
equipment
explosion
fire-hydrant
helicopter
helmet
incident
inhale
investigate
obstacle
officer
operation
oxygen
prevention
pursue

rapid response
report
rescue
risky
service
siren
squad car
station
successful
suspicious
temperature
valuable
volunteer
weapon
worthwhile

My own words

A couple of bright sparks!

Have you today used something that is powered by electricity? Maybe you have switched on a light, watched the television, used a computer or even used a kettle to make a cup of tea for your parents this morning! Today, in our modern **technological** world, we take it for granted that our homes and places of work have a regular, safe supply of electricity but that has not always been the case. We are able to enjoy the benefits of safe electricity because of the **inventions** and discoveries of scientists. Two of the most important early **pioneers** in this field were an American, Benjamin Franklin, and an Englishman, Michael Faraday. Our lives would not be as they are if it were not for the tireless work they did many years ago.

These two remarkable men had an immense curiosity about the natural world and were always trying to discover more about it. They both wanted to know how things worked and why they worked. They were good thinkers and problem solvers and carried out **experiments** to prove their ideas or to find out more. They became very famous and their work influenced scientists from all over the world. Yet they both came from humble beginnings and had little education. They were able to overcome these disadvantages and rose to positions of great influence in the scientific world. They were friends of royalty and powerful **politicians** but never forgot their humble beginnings.

Benjamin Franklin

Benjamin Franklin was born in Boston in the United States of America in 1706. He was the youngest of 17 children and the family did not have much money. His father ran his own soap shop but with so many mouths to feed life was always a struggle for the family. Benjamin did not go to school until he was eight years old. Up until that age his father had taught him in the little time he could spare from working in his shop. His father recognised in his son a thirst for knowledge and saved hard so he could send him to school. Benjamin went to school for three years but then his parents couldn't afford to send him anymore. At the age of 11 he joined his brother in his printing business and for the next nine years he learned all about the printing trade. During this time

Benjamin never stopped reading as much as he could about science and eventually he left his brother's business and set off for the large city of Philadelphia, determined to make something more of his life. He had almost no money, no job and only a loaf of bread to eat. However, he soon found a job and settled down with a new wife. Then he wrote a book that was to change his life. It became a best seller and he became very rich.

Benjamin was now able to concentrate on the things that really interested him. He became a public figure and a politician as well as a successful business man. He travelled all over Europe meeting royalty and famous people of the day. But his greatest interest was in science and he carried out many experiments, particularly to do with static electricity. This is electricity that is

Benjamin Franklin's experiment with lightning.

not usually moving, but is still or stationary. Scientists had not yet discovered how to make electricity move or how to control it. He thought that lightning might be an example of moving electricity and wanted to prove it. He discovered that lightning was attracted to metal so he came up with the idea of a **lightning conductor** which was a device that would attract the lightning and pass it safely down to the ground so that buildings did not catch fire. However, he needed to prove his ideas were correct, so in 1752 he conducted an experiment that made

him even more famous. It was a very dangerous thing to do and he was lucky not to be killed. He went out in a storm and flew a kite with metal rods attached. He hoped the electricity in the thunderclouds would be attracted to the rods and travel down the string, which was wet from the rain, onto a metal key attached to the string. It did and a spark jumped from the key into a special 'electrical jar' used to store electricity. A little later another scientist tried the same experiment and was killed! As a result of his experiment Benjamin invented the first lightning conductor and it was soon in use on buildings all over America.

After this he spent most of his time involved in politics but still managed to invent **bifocal spectacles** and a fireplace that heated rooms much more efficiently. In fact this last invention was so successful he could have made a second fortune from it, but he said that it was for the benefit of all and he didn't want to make money from it. He became one of the most influential Americans of his time and famous all over Europe. He died in 1790, but will always be remembered more for his scientific discoveries concerning electricity than for his politics.

Franklin's stove

Michael Faraday

A year later Michael Faraday was born. He is famous for discovering how to make electricity move and for inventing the first electric motor. Like Benjamin he was born into a poor family. He was one of five children and his father was a **blacksmith** in Surrey, England. His childhood was difficult and for a long time he only had one loaf of bread a week to live on. His parents were very religious and believed in 'simple living and high thinking', and this was the greatest influence on his life. He received almost no education and was essentially self-taught, learning to read, write and do simple maths. At the age of 13 he started to work for a bookseller where he took the opportunity to read as many books about science as he could.

He made notes about what he read and decided that what he wanted more than anything was to become a scientist. He wrote to the Royal Society, the most important group of scientists in the country, and asked for a job. They didn't even bother to reply to his letters, but this didn't stop him from carrying out his own experiments. Eventually he had the lucky break he needed. The president of the Royal Society, Sir Humphry Davy, had injured his eye and couldn't do any practical work and his assistant had just left. He remembered Michael's letters and asked him to work for him. Michael was thrilled and made the most of this opportunity. However, the post did not pay very much and he found he had to take odd jobs as well so he could keep himself and his wife.

He knew all about Benjamin Franklin's experiments with electricity and carried out some of his own trying to make and control the movement of electricity. In 1831 he built the first electric motor using a magnet that moved in and out of a coil of wire. At last it was possible to make electricity for ourselves and control it by switching it on and off. Eventually 50 years later this type of motor, called a dynamo, would be used in the world's first power station built in south-east England. This enabled electricity to be supplied to houses and businesses and replaced gas lights and steam engines. It was such a huge success that soon other power stations were built, not only in England but all over the world.

Soon Michael became a **celebrity** in England and was offered many important jobs in universities. He was a popular speaker and gave lectures and demonstrations all over England. He entertained Queen Victoria and her husband, Prince Albert, with his talks and his ability to explain difficult ideas in a way ordinary people could understand. He wanted children to become interested and excited by science and every Christmas he gave a series of lectures for children at the Royal Society. Lectures in his name, but given by famous scientists of today, still take place at Christmas and are often **televised**.

He was offered many honours and rewards for his work but he refused them, living a **frugal** and simple life. In 1839 he became ill and for six years was unable to do any work at all. He never really recovered from this illness and his health gradually became worse so that he couldn't even read or write. In 1858 Queen Victoria offered him a house in Hampton Court and a knighthood in recognition of his contribution to the world of science. He refused the knighthood but accepted the house, where he lived with his wife until his death in 1867. He was a modest man and left instructions that when he died he did not want a big public funeral but a simple family one. His headstone reads simply – Michael Faraday born 1791 died 1867.

Queen Victoria and Prince Albert

Our modern world is dependent on the supply of regular, safe electricity and we owe it all to these two great scientists. They were essentially self-taught men who were determined not to let their poor beginnings stop them from advancing in the world. They studied hard and spent a lot of time thinking about the world around them and trying to solve problems. Even though they both became famous they did not forget that their work would help everyone, rich or poor, and their lives were dedicated to helping others through the search for new knowledge and ideas.

Glossary
Bifocal spectacles – spectacles that have two types of lenses combined.
One is to help the wearer read things close to them; the other to see things further away.
Blacksmith – someone who makes things from iron, like horse shoes and farming tools.
Celebrity – someone who is famous.
Experiments – a test to discover or prove something.
Frugal – not wasting money or not spending much money.
Invention – a thing that has not been thought of or made before.
Lightning conductor – a strip of metal attached to the sides of tall buildings to channel the lightning safely down to earth and prevent fires.
Pioneers – people who do things first or discover things first.
Politics – the art of government.
Politician – someone who is involved in the work of the government (politics).
Technological – adjective from the noun 'technology' which is the application of science and mechanics.
Televised – something shown on television.

Bibliography
Bunce, Vincent, *Restless Planet – Volcanoes*, Wayland, 2000
Chambers, Catherine, *Disasters in Nature – Volcanoes*, Heinemann, 2000
Lafferty, Peter and Rowe, Julian, *The Inventor Through History*, Wayland Publishers, 1998
Parker, Steve, *Benjamin Franklin and Static Electricity*, Belitha Press, 1995

Understanding the grammar and punctuation

Pronouns

Pronouns are words used to replace nouns.

They are used by writers to avoid repeating the noun too often, particularly proper nouns (the names of people and places).

He wanted children to become interested and excited by science and every Christmas <u>he</u> gave a series of lectures for children at the Royal Society.

This sentence uses the pronoun 'he' to replace the name of the person being written about (Michael Faraday). It reads more easily than if it had been written without the pronouns as in the following example.

Michael Faraday wanted children to become interested and excited by science and every Christmas <u>Michael Faraday</u> gave a series of lectures for children at the Royal Society.

There are several kinds of pronouns including:

Personal pronouns : *I, me , he, him, she, her, we, us, they, them, it*

Possessive pronouns; *mine, yours, his, ours, theirs, its*

Relative pronouns: *who, whom, which, that*

Commas

Commas divide the different parts of a sentence to help make the meaning clear.

They can be used to separate items in a list.

Maybe you have switched on a light, watched the television, used a computer or even used a kettle to make a cup of tea for your parents in the morning!

They can be used to make a pause in a sentence.

He wrote to the Royal Society, the most important group of scientists in the country, and asked for a job.

Name

Pronouns

Rewrite the following sentences by replacing the underlined noun with a pronoun.

1. *The boy was watching television when the television blew up!*

   _____

2. *Benjamin did not go to school until Benjamin was eight years old.*

   _____

3. *Simon and Kamahl went to visit Mr Weston.*

   _____

4. *Sarah gave the ball back to Michael and Tom.*

   _____

The sentences below all contain at least one pronoun, but they are rather confusing!
For example, in the following sentence the pronoun 'it' is used but it isn't clear if it
was the cake or the loaf of bread that didn't taste very nice.

   He baked a cake and a loaf of bread but it did not taste very nice.

Now read each of these and think about why each one is unclear.

1. *Although the car hit the wall, it was not damaged.*

2. *We played with their ball and racquet as they were lying around the playground.*

3. *The Christmas holidays are coming soon, which is exciting.*

4. *They put their feet on the chairs and made them dirty.*

On the back of this sheet, write each sentence in your own words so the meaning is clear.

Name

Commas

Write these sentences again putting commas in to separate the items listed in each sentence. Remember not to write all the 'ands' except for the last one.

1. On my birthday I was given a football and a book and a CD and a set of pens and some money.

   _____

   _____

2. Yesterday I went into town and visited the library and the swimming baths and the park and the book shop.

   _____

   _____

3. The members of my swimming team are Julie and Karen and Parvinder and Lorna.

   _____

4. Before I could use my bike I had to mend the puncture in the rear tyre and oil the chain and adjust the handle bars.

   _____

   _____

5. When I get home from school I get changed and wash my hands then watch television and then I do my homework.

   _____

   _____

In these sentences the commas have been missed out. They are used to make a pause in the sentence. Put the commas in the correct places.

1. I joined the local library which is close to my home and go there every Saturday.

2. Our hotel the biggest in the resort was close to the beach.

3. The fishing trawler already loaded with fish ran into trouble when the storm blew up.

4. The computer which was only three months old stopped working after my little brother used it.

5. Smoking the biggest cause of cancer kills thousands of people every year.

Helpful hints for writing comparative reports

Research

✦ Find out as much as you can about the topic by researching different sources. Try to use a wide range of sources such as:
- reference books;
- text books;
- magazines;
- CD-Roms;
- the Internet;
- interviewing people.

Planning your text and note taking

✦ When doing your research, decide what different areas of the topic you are going to write about and write headings for them.

✦ As you make your notes write them under the appropriate headings. This will help you organise them. Write them as bullet points.

✦ Now decide how many paragraphs you will need and put them into order. Remember the first one should be a general introduction to the topic; and the last one should be a short summary of all the main points.

✦ Decide where you will place any diagrams or illustrations you wish to include in your report.

✦ Write each paragraph in draft form using your notes to help you. Start each paragraph with an opening sentence that tells the reader what it is about.

Editing your text

✦ Check your draft text for spelling or grammatical errors.

✦ Ensure you have used specialist vocabulary or technical terms if appropriate.

✦ Check that all illustrations or diagrams have captions and labels.

Comparing and contrasting

✦ When carrying out your research make a note of any similarities between your subjects. For example, if writing about two people include their ages, education, background, how they died and so on. These topics could help you form the opening sentences of paragraphs.

Both came from poor homes...

They were both interested in...

✦ Also note any obvious differences between your two subjects; for example, their education, the support or opportunities they had.

A did not benefit from a good education like B did...

Whereas A had the support of wealthy backers, B had to find all the money he needed himself.

Comparative reports
Scaffold 1

You are going to write a report comparing the lives and achievements of two famous pioneering aviators.

To help you plan your writing, use the framework below.

Choose one option from each stage, or use your own ideas.

Stage One

Below are some notes about two famous aviators.

Amelia Earhart
- Born 1897, Kansas USA
- Served as military nurse during WW1
- Obtained pilot's licence 1922
- Worked as teacher
- 1928 became first woman to cross the Atlantic by air
- 1935 became first person to fly from Hawaii to California
- 1937 mysteriously disappeared while trying to be the first person to fly around the world

Bessie Coleman
- Born Texas USA, 1892
- Aged 23 decided to learn to fly but not able to in USA because she was black
- 1920 set off for France to learn to fly
- 1921 obtained pilot's licence
- Performed at various air shows
- Died 1926 in flying accident

Now carry out your own research to find out more about their lives and achievements.

Use the library, the Internet and CD-Roms to read as much as you can about each of them.

Stage Two

Use the contents pages and indexes to find information about the following areas of your subject:

- their childhood
- their flying achievements
- their jobs
- how they died

Use these headings to organise your notes for each aviator as you make them:

1. Early life
2. Learning to fly
3. Achievements
4. How they died
5. Why they are remembered

Stage Three

Write a short introduction about the two women.

Start your introduction with one of the following phrases:

a) Today any adult can learn to fly but that has not always been the case.

b) The history of flight is dominated by famous men but two women deserve a special place in this history.

c) Have you ever wanted to learn to fly?

d) Today we are able to fly all over the world but 100 years ago we were only just beginning to build aircraft and learn how to fly.

Stage Four

Write several paragraphs about Amelia Earhart's life.

Use your notes for what you write under each heading.

Start each paragraph with a sentence that informs the reader what it is about.

Use ideas from the following:

a) Amelia Earhart was born in Kansas, USA in 1897. Her childhood was...

b) It was during her time as a military nurse in the First World War that Amelia…

c) Amelia obtained her pilot's licence in 1922. It was an amazing feat for a woman during those times and she went on to…

d) Several years later in 1928, Amelia Earhart became the first woman to fly across the Atlantic.

e) Amelia's death is still surrounded by mystery and controversy…

Stage Five

Write several paragraphs about Bessie Coleman's life.

Use your notes for what you write under each heading.

Start each paragraph with a sentence that informs the reader what it is about.

Use similar ideas as those for Amelia (see Stage 4).

Stage Six

Write a short concluding paragraph to summarise the main points from your text.

Choose from these opening sentences or write your own.

a) Amelia and Bessie were both pioneering woman but for different reasons.

b) Both woman will be remembered for leading the way for other woman in a man's world.

c) Although both women died tragically they will always be remembered for their bravery.

Comparative reports
Vocabulary bank 1

accident	difficult	pilot
achievement	disappeared	pioneers
aeroplane	experience	remarkable
aircraft	extraordinary	remembered
air shows	flying	special
amazing	France	struggle
Atlantic	history	teacher
aviator	important	travel
biplane	learn	woman/ women
childhood	lesson	world
compass	licence	
determined	nurse	

My own words

Comparative reports
Scaffold 2

You are going to write about the lives and achievements of two famous people.
To help you plan your report, use the framework below.
Choose one option from each stage, or use your own ideas.

Stage One

Choose from the following pairs of famous people.

a) Henry VIII and Queen Victoria;

b) Jessie Owens and Mohammed Ali;

c) Martin Luther King and John Lennon.

Carry out your own research to find out about their lives
and achievements.

Use the library, the Internet and CD-Roms to read as much
as you can about each of them.

Stage Two

Use the contents pages and indexes to find information about the following areas of your subject:

- their childhood;

- their early adult life and any struggles or
   difficulties they had;

- their main achievements;

- the end of their lives (if they have died);

- their legacy (what they will be/are
   remembered for).

Use these headings to organise your notes for
each person as you make them:

- childhood

- early adulthood

- achievements

- legacy

Stage Three

Write a short introduction about the two people. Write about the things that link them together.

Start your introduction with one of the following (or use your own ideas).

a) History has presented us with many tales of fascinating kings and queens of England but Henry VIII and Queen Victoria are amongst the best remembered.

b) The world of sport has given rise to some amazing sportsmen and women but two who stand out from the rest are Jessie Owens and Mohammed Ali.

c) Martin Luther King and John Lennon were very different people and yet they have many things in common, including the fact that they were both tragically assassinated.

Stage Four

Write several paragraphs about the first person's life. Then several about the second person's life.

Use your notes to help you write under each heading.
Start each paragraph with a sentence that informs the reader what it is about.
Use ideas from the following:

a) Henry VIII is most remembered for his six wives but his early life was…

b) Queen Victoria's long reign began in 1837 when she came to the throne after…

c) Jessie Owen was the first American to win four gold medals in the track and field events in a single Olympic Games.

d) Mohammed Ali began his boxing career at the tender age of 12…

e) John Lennon grew up in Liverpool in England. He lived with his…

f) Martin Luther King was born in 1929 in Atlanta, Georgia, USA. He was the second child…

Stage Five

Write a short concluding paragraph to summarise the main points from your text. Remember to link this back to your opening introductory paragraph.

You can use one of the following to start your paragraph or write one of your own:

a) X and Y will be/are best remembered for…

b) Although X and Y came from very different backgrounds they both achieved…

c) The world of sport owes much to these two famous sportsmen who…

d) Born a world apart and following totally different life styles these two men will both be remembered for their unrelenting campaigns for world peace.

Comparative reports
Vocabulary bank 2

achievement
admired
America/American
assassination
athletics
background
campaign
childhood
determination
difficulties
England/English
famous
incredible
international

medals
mourning
musician
Nobel Peace Prize
Olympics
outstanding
Parkinson's Disease
peace
powerful
preacher
recognition
reign
remembered
similar

special
spectators
struggle
successful
throne
tradition
tremendous
unique
world
writer
youngest

My own words

What are volcanoes?

Who could argue that one of the most devastating natural forces on Earth is the volcano? An erupting volcano is a spectacular but deadly sight. It can shoot red-hot **lava**, ash, rocks and steam high into the atmosphere causing tremendous devastation across a wide area. When these deadly substances cool they form new landscapes and a volcanic **cone** rises above the ground. The natural world around the volcano may be destroyed and often there is a loss of human life as well. Quite simply, an erupting volcano is a natural disaster on a massive scale.

To begin to understand how volcanoes are formed you need to know the structure of Earth. Earth has three main layers. The surface is called the **crust**, which is made up of solid rock, and it can vary in thickness. In some places it may be quite thick – up to 60km underneath the highest mountain chains – and in others it may be very thin and weak. Directly beneath the crust is the **mantle**, which is a thick layer of **molten** rock called **magma**. And finally, at the centre is the **core** which has an outer liquid layer and a solid centre.

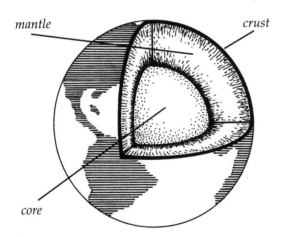

mantle   crust

core

Think of Earth as a huge ball of fiery hot molten rock covered with a relatively thin skin of cool, hard rock. Because heat always rises the hot magma is constantly trying to find a way upwards and when it finds a particularly thin area of crust, or a crack in the crust, it will escape through it. This action of escaping is called erupting.

However, it would be wrong to think that volcanoes are always erupting. Sometimes they will lie **dormant**, or inactive, for years – even centuries. When the hot lava and ash cool they become solid and hard. This plugs the gap in the Earth's crust and the magma can no longer escape until enough pressure builds up again beneath the plug. Eventually the plug is ejected with enormous force.

This explosive force is created because a lot of energy is released through a small opening, as with any explosion. What escapes through the gap is different according to the amount of force behind the eruption. Sometimes there may be only a small amount of force in which case small puffs of ash or gases are released causing little damage. On other occasions there may be more energy forcing runny lava to flow out and spread out across the sides of the volcano. Because these lava flows travel relatively slowly they rarely cause harm to humans but will damage or destroy any wildlife or property they come into contact with.

The most destructive and violent eruptions occur when the magma is mixed with large amounts of gases. The power of the eruption can be so great that huge areas of the volcano itself can be blown away. Pieces of rock and magma are blasted out with tremendous force shooting hundreds, or even thousands of metres, into the air. As these pieces cool in the air they become more solid and are called **volcanic bombs.** They can weigh up to100 tonnes! In addition to these bombs, a giant cloud of ash and dust is spurted into the air. This cloud can travel great distances and spread over a wide area. It can hang in the air for a long time making it difficult for people and animals to breathe. Machinery is clogged up and buildings may collapse under the weight of the dust and ash when it settles. It can form a blanket of fine ash and dust many metres thick that can completely swamp an area or towns and villages. Sometimes the cloud is blasted so high into the air that it is carried along by jet streams of wind thousands of miles around the Earth.

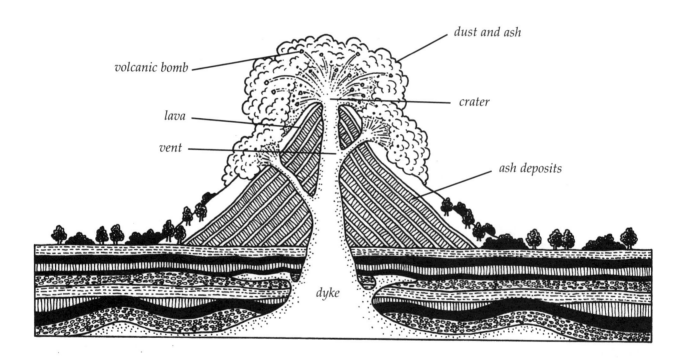

One of the most spectacular and devastating effects of an eruption is a huge sea wave called a **Tsunami**. These occur when the eruption causes the waters of neighbouring seas to move suddenly. Then the surface of the sea swells and forms large waves. These waves become taller, faster and more powerful as they travel across the surface of the sea. They can travel at up to speeds of 800kph and be as tall as a block of flats. When they hit a shoreline they cause the most destructive damage to property and often a massive loss of life.

Although initially volcanic eruptions are destructive in their nature they can also be creative in the longer term. The volcanic soil around volcanoes is very fertile for growing crops and feeding animals. New landscapes are formed as are new rocks, called igneous rocks. And finally, even though we are not able to predict eruptions with any accuracy and they cause so much devastation, we have learned to harness the power and heat from them. This heat and steam is used in some areas to create electricity in small power stations, and these provide electricity for the local towns and villages.

So, you can see we cannot prevent eruptions, and we are often profoundly affected by their destructive power, but at least we have found a way of turning this extraordinary raw power to our advantage.

GLOSSARY[25]

Cone – the rounded and pointed shape of many volcanoes.

Core – Earth's centre in the form of a ball made of very hot metal.

Crust – the outer layer of Earth, which is hard.

Dormant – an adjective to describe a 'sleeping' volcano which has not erupted for many years.

Igneous rocks – rocks that come from under the crust and are formed by intense heat.

Lava – molten rock that flows from a volcano across Earth's surface.

Magma – melted rock under the Earth's surface.

Mantle – a layer inside Earth, between the core and crust.

Molten – an adjective to describe a rock that is heated until it melts.

Tsunami – a huge sea wave.

Volcanic bombs – a lump of volcanic rock thrown from a volcano that cools and becomes rounded.

Bibliography[26]

Bunce, Vincent, *Restless Planet – Volcanoes*, Wayland, 2000

Chambers, Catherine, *Disasters in Nature – Volcanoes*, Heinemann, 2000

Green, Jen, *A Closer Look at: Volcanoes*, Franklin Watts, 1998

Martin, Fred, *Focus on Disasters*, Heinemann, 1995

Understanding the grammar and punctuation

Cause and effect

In explanatory texts the writer may want to explain why something occurs. This is called cause and effect.

This explosive force is created <u>because</u> a lot of energy is released through a small opening...

Here the writer is explaining that the force of energy through a small opening (the cause) creates an explosion (the effect).

Linking words (connectives) are often used to join the cause and effect in a sentence.

if, then, when, why, consequently, because, so, therefore, as a result

Using punctuation to get the reader's attention

Sometimes a writer wants to make a sentence stand out in order to grab the reader's attention.

Who could argue that one of the most devastating natural forces on Earth is the volcano?

By making this sentence a question, the writer speaks to the reader directly.

They can weigh up to 100 tonnes!

An exclamation mark (!) gives this sentence greater emphasis.

*And finally, at the centre is the **core** which has an outer liquid layer and a solid centre.*

The use of **bold text** draws attention to an important word.

Cause and effect

The following sentences have been cut up. Match each part so that they make a complete sentence. You will need to add a linking word to some of them.
Use words like – as, so, when, then, because and by.

The heavy snow fall caused	the antelope managed to escape
When the stage lights came on	it saw them approaching her cubs
The howling wind raged outside	an electrical fault
My younger brother was crying	the roof to collapse
I was late for the start of the match	bought a new game for the computer
The fire was started	she bandaged my cut hand
The lion went hungry that day	he was blinded for a moment
The bear attacked	the crew got little sleep that night
I saved up all my pocket money	my tyre had a slow puncture
When the nurse came	he wasn't allowed to watch television

Now underline the words that show the cause in red and the effect in blue.

Write TWO cause and effect sentences of your own.

1. _____

_____

2. _____

_____

Question marks and exclamation marks

Read these sentences and decide if there should be a question mark or an exclamation mark at the end of each one. Write it in.

1. Did you know that the first submarine was built in 1620

2. Humans sleep for approximately one third of their lives

3. Our next door neighbour gave birth to quadruplets last week

4. I'm going to Disney World for Christmas

5. Who would have thought I would be made captain of the school quiz team

6. The bush fire raged for 20 days before it was finally put out

7. When the plane flew over our house the window panes rattled

8. Have you ever wondered why the sky is blue

Using bold lettering

Read these sentences and decide which word in each one is the most important and should be in bold lettering to draw the reader's attention to it. Underline the word that should be in bold.

1. The brain is the most complex organ in the body.

2. Use a thermometer to measure how hot it is outside.

3. An estuary is the widest part of a river.

4. You can now buy digital cameras that don't need film to record the picture.

5. It is possible to watch live television pictures from around the world using a satellite to bounce the pictures from one country to another.

Helpful hints for writing explanations

Explanations are written to explain the way things are or how they work.

Collecting information

✦ Research your subject carefully and collect information from a variety of sources. Use books, magazines, CD-roms and the Internet. Make notes of important facts and details you find. Make a note of the sources you used because you should list these at the end of your text.

Organising your text

✦ Begin your text with an opening statement that introduces the topic. Follow this with a series of steps in a logical order. Each step could form a different paragraph and explain how something works, or why something happens. Make sure that you link each area of information to show cause and effect. Continue until the final state is produced or the explanation is complete. You may want to finish by writing a short paragraph that gives an explanation of the value of the process.

✦ You could write about:
- why it is useful;
- why it is successful;
- how it helps us.

Language features

✦ Start your text with a title that indicates what the subject is about. It can be in the form of a question to interest the reader immediately and inform them that the text will answer this question.

✦ Use appropriate subject specific terms and technical vocabulary. You can explain what these mean as you use them or in a glossary at the end of the text.

✦ Remember to write in an impersonal style in the simple present tense.

Glossary

✦ Any technical or subject specific words used in the text that the reader may not know the meaning of should be explained in a glossary at the end of the text. Remember to indicate these words can be found in the glossary by writing them in bold print.

Illustrations/diagrams

✦ Include illustrations or diagrams to help explain processes or difficult ideas.

✦ Think about where in the text they should be placed. Make sure that you label them and add detail using short descriptions of what is happening.

Explanations
Scaffold 1

You are going to write an explanation about a process in the natural world.
To help plan your writing, use the framework below.
Choose options from each stage as appropriate.

Stage One

Research one of the following.

a) How rivers are formed and change over their course.
b) The features of coasts and how they are formed.
c) The features of mountains and how they are formed.

Use as many sources of information as you can. Use the library, the Internet and CD-Roms. Read as much as you can about your chosen subject. Make a note of all the sources you use.

Stage Two

Make notes on some of the following areas of information and use them for a paragraph plan.

a) What is a river / coast / mountain?

b) What are the common features of rivers / coasts / mountains?

c) How are these features formed?

d) How do humans use rivers / coasts / mountains?

Stage Three

Write a short introduction about your chosen subject.
Choose one of these openings:

a) Have you ever wondered how rivers are formed?
b) Rivers are one of the most striking natural features of landscapes.
c) All rivers, whether they be large or small, begin in a humble way.
d) Have you ever walked beneath a cliff and wondered how it was formed?
e) Coasts range from dramatic, wave battered shores to sandy beaches.
f) Coasts are the fragile boundary between the two different worlds of land and sea.
g) Do you know how mountains are formed?
h) Mountains are one of the most amazing landscape features of our world.
i) Mountains are magnificent landforms that dominate the areas surrounding them.

Stage Four

Use your paragraph plan to write about each area of your subject.

Start each paragraph with an opening sentence that informs the reader what the paragraph is about. Remember to link each paragraph together if you can by using some of these links:

a) Once this has happened…
b) When this happens…
c) After this…
d) As a result of…
e) The next stage is…
f) One of the differences between…
g) The effect of this is…
h) The most common of these…
i) Another stage in its formation is…
j) However, this is not always the case…
k) Although this happens…
l) So you can see…

WHICH SHALL I CHOOSE?

Stage Five

Draw a diagram to provide extra information or to make difficult ideas easier to understand.

Label your diagram. Think about where you will place it.
Your diagram might be about:
a) how a bend in a river is formed;
b) the features of coasts such a cliff, headland, beach, arch;
c) where the world's highest mountains are found.

Stage Six

Write a short conclusion to your explanation.

This should sum up what you have written or give an overall evaluation of the subject.
Try using one of these:

a) So as you can see rivers/coasts/mountains are…
b) Finally…
c) If we are to continue to enjoy our rivers/coasts/mountains then…
d) These wonders of nature…
e) The pleasure rivers/coast/mountains provide can not be measured.
f) However, if we do not protect these wonders…

Write a bibliography of all the sources of information you have used.
Write a glossary of technical words used in the text.

Explanations
Vocabulary bank 1

Rivers

bank
channel
course
current
deposit
downstream
erode/erosion
estuary
flood plain
flow
meander
ox-bow lake
rapid
rise/rising
shallow
source
spring
steep
stream
tributary
upstream
valley
widens

Coasts

arch
bay
beach
boulders
cave
cliffs
collapse
dunes
headland
inlet
pebbles
rocks/rocky
sandy
shingle
shore/shoreline
stack
tide
waves

Mountains

base
climate
climb/climbers
conservation
fault
fold
highest
metres
peak
plateau
range
recreation
summit
tourists
vegetation
world

My own words

Explanations
Scaffold 2

You are going to write an explanation about how different parts of the body work.
To help plan your writing, use the framework below.
Choose options from each stage as appropriate, or use your own ideas.

Stage One

Choose one of the following:

a) How our eyes enable us to see.
b) How our bodies use food to keep us healthy.
c) How our heart works.

Research your chosen subject using a wide range of
sources of information. You can use books, CD-Roms,
the Internet or talk to someone who knows a lot about
the subject.

Stage Two

Make notes on some of the following areas of information and use them for a paragraph plan.

a) **Eyes**: why we need to see; how the eye sees images; how the images are sent to the brain; what the brain does with these images it receives.
b) **Food/eating**: why we need to eat; how the mouth begins the process of eating; how the stomach processes food; the role of different organs in processing food; how our bodies dispose of waste products.
c) **Heart**: what a heart is; how it sends blood; how it receives blood; heart problems.

Stage Three

Write a short introduction to your text. It should provide an overall view of the subject. Make it interesting.

You could start with one of the following or write your own beginning.

a) Our eyes are one of the ways in which we can explore our world.
b) Our eyes are one of our vital organs.
c) Sometimes we take food for granted, but without it we would all die.
d) The way our bodies process food is fascinating.
e) The heart is one of our most important organs.
f) The heart is an amazing machine.

Stage Four

Use your paragraph plan (Stage 2) to write about different aspects of your subject.

Each paragraph should explain a particular area of information. Each one will provide specific details of how the body parts work.

Try using some of these paragraph links:
a) This explains why...
b) Therefore we need to...
c) Consequently our bodies need to...
d) As a result of this...
e) This causes...
f) So in order to stay healthy we need to...

Stage Five

Draw a diagram of either: the eye, the heart or the digestive system. Label it.

You may choose to draw other diagrams showing more detail of each part of the organ or process. For example:

Eyes
a) The front of the eye

b) The optic nerve

c) The brain

Digestive system
a) The stomach

b) The intestines

c) The kidney

The heart
a) The arteries

b) The veins

Stage Six

Write a short conclusion to summarise the role and importance of your chosen subject.
Use one of the following to begin your conclusion or write your own.

a) Therefore, it is clear that without our eyes/hearts/food...
b) So as you can see...
c) Finally...
d) Without our eyes/hearts/digestive system we would not...

Write a glossary of technical terms.
Write a bibliography of the sources of information you have used.

Explanations
Vocabulary bank 2

Eyes	Digestive system	Heart
cornea	absorb	artery
fibres	acid	beat
focus	bladder	blood
function	chew	chamber
image	diet	circulate
inverted	digest	circulation
iris	dissolve	direction
lens	healthy	flow
light	intestine	force
nerve	kidneys	muscle
object	liver	pressure
optic nerve	nutrients	pulse
organ	oesophagus	pump
pupil	passes	vein
sight	rectum	vessels
socket	saliva	vital
sphere	stomach	
	swallow	
	teeth	
	throat	

My own words

RIVERSIDE THEME PARK

THE MOST TECHNOLOGICALLY ADVANCED THEME PARK IN THE WORLD

THE THRILLS NEVER END

VOTED BEST THEME PARK IN THE WORLD
('TEEN TIMES' READERS' POLL)

*At Riverside Park we guarantee everyone will have a day they will never forget. Whether you are 6 or 60 we have something for you.
Our specialist team of engineers and scientists have created the newest and most advanced technological designs to bring you the very best adventure rides and attractions to be found anywhere in the world.*

**Thrill seekers, seen the rest?
Come and visit the very best!**

NEW FOR THIS YEAR

DROP ZONE
RIDE IT IF YOU DARE
THE WORLD'S TALLEST TOWER DROP

Riverside Park is the most unique theme park in the world.
We have over 200 rides and attractions that will leave you breathless
and open-mouthed with awe and wonder.

The park is divided into different zones, each with its own theme.

SKY ZONE – rocket-powered thrusting thrills

Probably the highest and fastest rides anywhere in the world.

DROP ZONE – new this year

APOLLO ADVENTURE – out of this world

THE BLACK HOLE – so scary we can't let you see where you're going!

SPLASH DOWN – white-water wonders

Water rides that will leave you gasping for breath.

WHITE WATER CANYON – not for the fainthearted

STORM – can you survive the storm?

WHIRLPOOL – with an amazing reverse drop

NEED FOR SPEED – white-knuckle roller-coasters

Cork screws, loops, drops – we've got the lot!

FIRESTORM – our fastest ride!

JET STREAM – stand up if you dare!

DRAGSTER – who needs brakes?

For those of you who like to take things a little slower why not visit our incredible interactive rides and attractions? There's the ANIMAL KINGDOM, PIRATES' ISLAND, THE FAIRGROUND and many, many more.

**And if after all the excitement you feel the need for a rest or refreshments, we have
FIVE RESTAURANTS and bars catering for all tastes. Over TWENTY KIOSKS provide
ice-creams, hot and cold drinks and fast food.
Why not visit one of our FOUR SHOPS where you can buy souvenirs of your visit?**

Admission prices

Family ticket (2 adults & 2 children): £100

Adults: £ 35

Children (under12): £25

New for this year
WHEN YOU RIDE ON ATTRACTIONS MARKED WITH
A STAR REMEMBER TO GET YOUR PASS STAMPED.
IF YOU VISIT ALL OF THEM ON ONE DAY YOU GET
20% OFF YOUR ADMISSION PRICE NEXT TIME YOU
VISIT RIVERSIDE PARK.

(SEE NOTICES AT ENTRANCE FOR FURTHER DETAILS)

Understanding the grammar and punctuation

Using strong verbs

Writers use strong verbs in order to make the statement stand out from other sentences.

Water rides that will leave you <u>gasping</u> for breath.

The word 'gasping' is very descriptive and is a much stronger verb than 'puffing' or 'panting', for example.

Using strong adjectives

Writers use strong adjectives in order to make descriptions more exciting.

<u>Incredible interactive</u> rides

...leave you <u>breathless</u> and <u>open-mouthed</u>...

<u>rocket-powered thrusting</u> thrills

Alliteration

An alliteration is where a sequence of words begins with the same letter to make the message or title more memorable.

White-water wonders

Thrusting thrills

Puns

A pun is a play on words. They have a double meaning.

Apollo Adventure – <u>out of this world</u>.

Here the author is comparing a theme park ride to the Apollo spacecraft which actually *does* travel out of this world.

Exclamation marks (!)

Advertisements often use exclamation marks at the end of statements or commands to show excitement or wonder.

Stand up if you dare!

So scary we can't let you see where you're going!

Verbs

Replace the underlined verbs in these sentences with 'stronger' ones to give the sentence more impact and interest. The first one has been done for you.

1.   Ross <u>got</u> out of bed because he was late for school. Ross <u>scurried</u> out of bed because he was late for school.

2.   The storm clouds <u>moved</u> across the darkening sky as we <u>walked</u> back to the car.

     _____

3.   The fireworks <u>went</u> high into the night sky and <u>fell</u> back to earth in a shower of colourful sparks.

     _____

     _____

4.   The children <u>stood</u> behind the wall and watched as the thieves <u>drove</u> away in their getaway car.

     _____

     _____

5.   Amy eagerly <u>walked</u> down the stairs to <u>eat</u> her birthday dinner.

     _____

Use a thesaurus to find some alternatives for these verbs. You may use verb phrases as well as single verbs. Select the ten 'strongest'.

take	*hit*	*mix*	*stay*
send	*stop*	*escape*	

Name

Exclamation marks

Read the sentences below. Add an exclamation mark to those
sentences that need one.

1. Our holiday was ruined by a hurricane.
2. The library was closed for redecoration.
3. Smoking kills.
4. Free entry if it's your birthday.
5. Danger quick sand.
6. Swim only if the yellow flag is flying.
7 . The summer fayre is on the 22nd.

Question marks

Read the sentences below. Add a question mark to those sentences that need one.

1. Ghost train – dare you to enter.
2. For those who like a thrill why not visit our roller coaster section.
3. Can you survive the fastest ride on Earth.
4. Never question our claims, we are always right.
5. Too afraid to take a chance.
6. Don't worry, we're here to help you.
7. Want to experience the fright of your life.

Now write three exclamations and three questions of your own that could be used as part of an
advertisement for Riverside Theme Park.

_____

_____

_____

_____

_____

Helpful hints for writing a leaflet

Catchy slogans

✦ Use short catchy phrases throughout your leaflet to make the message more memorable. Think of a really good one to go with the name of your product.

Riverside Theme Park – the most technologically advanced theme park in the world

Keep the text simple

✦ Use simple language that ensures the message is clear. Don't write too much. You want the reader to remember the key messages.

Make the leaflet visually appealing

✦ The overall look of your leaflet is important. It must instantly appeal to the reader. Use different colours and styles of lettering. Use different sizes of lettering. Change the angle of the writing so some of it slopes.

✦ Use text boxes to make some sections stand out on the page.

> **Admission prices**
>
> *Family ticket (2 adults & 2 children): £100*
>
> *Adults: £ 35*
>
> *Children (under12): £25*

✦ If you have access to a computer, try using a leaflet template that will print it out on different sides of the paper and allow the leaflet to be folded.

Use humour

✦ Use puns to make the slogans amusing and more memorable.

Fact and opinion

✦ Use a combination of facts and opinions in your leaflet. The reader will need to know some basic facts like: the cost of the product, where the product can be purchased, what the product does or contains.

✦ Offer opinions about how good the product is. These can be written to sound like facts by using words like 'probably'.

Probably the highest and fastest rides anywhere in the world.

Illustrations

✦ Add drawings, cartoons or photographs to your leaflet to catch the reader's attention and make them want to read the whole leaflet.

Endorsements

✦ Make your product seem really important or different by using quotes from people or organisations stating how good the product is.

Voted best theme park in the world ('Teen Times' readers' poll)

Incentives

✦ Offer incentives to the reader to make the product seem even more appealing or a bargain. Like – 'Only £1 this month' or 'free gift included'.

A leaflet
Scaffold 1

You are going to write a leaflet advertising a new magazine for children.
To help you write your leaflet, use the framework below.
Choose options from each stage as appropriate.

Stage One

Choose one of these types of magazines to make your leaflet about:

a) a new magazine about pets;

b) a new sports magazine;

c) a magazine about science and technology;

d) a music magazine.

You may find it helpful to choose the subject you are most interested in yourself.
Think about what it is about the subject that interests you.
Think about the magazines you like, and why you like them. What is it about the way they are produced that appeals to you personally?
Write a big, bold title.

Stage Two

**Draw a picture of the cover of your magazine.
Write a slogan to go with it.**

a) Buy (name of magazine) NOW! Or live to regret it.
b) OUT NOW! The ONLY magazine you will ever need.
c) Want to be up with the latest trends? Then buy (name of magazine) NOW!
d) Be COOL! Buy (name of magazine).
e) This mag beats the rest
   New and cool, it's the best!

Stage Three

Write some sentences about the magazine to tell the readers what it is about. Try to grab the reader's attention.

Tell them about:
a) who should buy the magazine – the age range;
b) how often the magazine comes out – monthly / weekly;
c) the price and where it can be bought;
d) why the magazine is different from all the rest;
e) why they should buy it.

Stage Four

Write a heading called: In this issue.

List the features that will included in your magazine.
Choose from:

a) help page to solve readers' problems;
b) crosswords, competitions and puzzles section;
c) hints and tips;
d) what's new? latest news and trends;
e) readers' letter page;
f) photo section.

Use bold letters and bright colours to make these features stand out in the leaflet.

Stage Five

Make two text boxes with important information inside.

Choose from:

a) a special offer for the reader;

b) a special event sponsored by the magazine;

c) a competition;

d) a quote from a famous person who recommends buying the magazine;

e) special facts about the magazine.

SPECIAL OFFER!
Get a friend to subscribe
and win a portable TV!

Stage Six

Add some drawings to your leaflet.

Choose from:

a) a famous person holding up the magazine in front of them;

b) a person doing a paper round where the sack is full of your magazine;

c) a person relaxing on a sun lounger, reading the magazine;

d) a cartoon character with a speech bubble saying how good the magazine is.

A leaflet
Vocabulary bank 1

advanced
amazing
articles
buy
comment
competition
contents
crossword
detailed
editor
expert
fantastic

features
guaranteed
guide
invaluable
knowledge
magazine
monthly
photographs
price
prizes
problem
publication

puzzles
reader
regular
report
review
sensational
series
special offer
subscribe
subscription
value for money
weekly

My own words

A leaflet
Scaffold 2

You are going to write a leaflet advertising your school. The purpose of the leaflet is to persuade parents to send their children to your school.

To help you write your leaflet, use the framework below.

Choose options from each stage as appropriate, or use your own ideas.

Stage One

Think about all the good things your school does for you and provides for you. Make a list of them. Make notes about:

a) the building and grounds (premises);
b) the classrooms and the things found in them (resources);
c) the teachers and the way they teach you (teaching and learning);
d) after school clubs, sports and other out of classroom activities you might do (extra-curriculum).

Draw four text boxes on the page with the following headings:
1. Premises
2. Resources
3. Teaching and learning
4. Extra-curriculum activities

Stage Two

Think of a slogan to go at the top or centre of your leaflet. It should summarise in a catchy way the very best reason for attending your school.

Examples might be:
a) (school name) where the children come first in everything;
b) (school name) where learning is fun;
c) You want the best for your child, so do we;
d) Want to be top of the class? Then come and meet us at (school name).

Now think of a catchy slogan or short phrase to go at the top of each text box. These should be eye-catching and easy to remember.

Try to use:
a) puns – a humourous play on words;
b) alliteration – where each word of the slogan begins with the same letter;
c) strong verbs and adjectives;
d) exclamations.

Stage Three

Now write the text for each text box.

Try to include important facts but also make them sound interesting by using descriptive and emotive language.

Use phrases like:
a) Here at (your school name) we provide…
b) Our bright, modern building…
c) Our dedicated staff…
d) The spacious classrooms…
e) Spectacular grounds provide…
f) Well equipped classrooms…
g) We achieve amazing results by…

Stage Four

Next think about the illustrations you will use to make your leaflet visually appealing.

Each text box could have an illustration.
It should be clear and to do with the theme of each box.

Your illustrations could show:
a) features of the school grounds such as playground equipment, wildlife area;
b) the school hall and gymnastic equipment;
c) the school staff;
d) the layout of a classroom;
e) the library area.

Mr Brown Mrs King Mr Jones

Mrs Riettie Mr Field Miss Ball

Stage Five

Now add all the important facts such as:

a) full school address including post code;
b) contact telephone and fax numbers; school website address;
c) names of all staff;
d) school term dates;
e) school start and finish times plus break and lunch times;
f) timetable of after school/lunch time clubs;
g) calendar of annual events.

A leaflet
Vocabulary bank 2

accommodation
achievements
adults
advanced
after school
assemblies
awards
beautiful
behaviour
caring
comfortable
condition
considerable
discipline
during
education
enthusiastic
equipment

excellent
facilities
families
fantastic
grounds
headteacher
helpful
important
impressive
interesting
league
learning
lessons
library
lively
marvellous
modern
outstanding

playground
primary
pupils
reception
resources
results
secure
spacious
special
sport
staff
superb
surroundings
teacher/teaching
timetable
tradition
up-to-date
variety

My own words

A persuasive letter

Mrs. M. Bradley
54 Parkway Drive
Cartbridge
CA3 5DG

23rd March 2004

The Editor
Cartbridge Gazette
Victoria House
12 The High Street
Cartbridge
CA1 8RT

Dear Sir

I am writing to express my deep concern over the planned building of the new Cartbridge bypass, as reported in last week's edition of the Cartbridge Gazette, and to ask whether you and your paper would consider joining me in opposing its construction.

The construction of such a major project will bring disruption, pollution and noise to our quiet town and will destroy much of our cherished countryside.

I am opposed to the building of the bypass on several grounds. Firstly, we do not need one. Although it is true that the volume of traffic passing through our pleasant little town has increased in recent years, it has not increased to such a degree that it merits a bypass to be built. Surely the local council can devise a scheme for the town centre which is able to handle this small increase in traffic, such as widening the main road and installing traffic lights to regulate the flow. This would then avoid the ensuing disruption caused by noisy road building machinery while the bypass is being built.

Secondly, the traffic that travels through the town brings much needed revenue to the local shops and businesses. Many of the vehicles that travel through Cartbridge are on their way to the coast and often stop for a break in their journey. This benefits local cafes and shops especially during the summer months. If these vehicles drive past our town, they will be unaware of the many splendid facilities and services on offer to visitors. Many of them will lose vital customers; some even forced to close. Only last month your paper published an article regarding the concerns of the local Chamber of Commerce over the increasing number of businesses struggling to survive in the current economic climate. Therefore, it won't be just the tourists who suffer, we local residents will be deprived of these vital services also.

Thirdly, the proposed route of this unnecessary road cuts across some of our finest countryside. We need this countryside for both farming and recreation. Much of what we all value will be destroyed and lost for ever. There is particular concern about the road passing directly through Farnham Wood. If the road follows the proposed route, this wood will be completely destroyed. This ancient woodland at the north of the town has stood for centuries and benefited the town immensely. It has brought so much pleasure to local people over the years. You only have to take a stroll along its delightful paths on any given weekend to observe its popularity, especially with families. If the bypass is built, future generations will never have the opportunity to experience its many pleasures.

Furthermore, there is the matter of the wildlife that occupies the wood. What will become of the flora and fauna that flourish there? It is a valuable habitat for so many forms of animals, birds and plants. The Cartbridge Natural History Society's last annual report indicated that the wood is of particular scientific importance. The wood contains several badger setts, which are believed to be the last remaining in the county. In the spring several rare species of plants are to be found, in particular bluebells, which as your readers may know are now a protected species in some areas. A bypass through the wood will destroy both the setts and the bluebells and much more besides.

Therefore, it is my belief that the construction of a bypass will have a severe detrimental effect on the town and its residents. In short, local shops will suffer, recreational land will be lost and wildlife will be destroyed. Cartbridge will never be the same again. So I urge your paper and its readers to join me in opposing the project.

Yours faithfully

Mary Bradley

Mary Bradley

Understanding the grammar and punctuation

Prepositions

A preposition is a word or group of words that shows the relationship between a noun (or pronoun) and another word in a sentence.

They are often about time:

at two o'clock

during the holidays

on Saturday

They can also be about place:

under the stairs

near the door

Apostrophe of possession

An apostrophe (') is used to show belonging (possession).

last week's edition

...Natural History Society's last annual report

If the word is plural and already ends in an 's', the apostrophe is added to the end of the word:

the teachers' staffroom

the boys' toilets

Capital letters for proper nouns

Capital letters are used for the names of people, places, titles, organisations, days, months and so on.

Cartbridge

Cartbridge Gazette

Mary Bradley

54 Parkway Drive

Cartbridge Natural History Society

Prepositions

Choose the most appropriate prepositions from the box below to complete these sentences.

beneath	across	before	near	over	under
behind	along	for	with	during	to
until	by	at	between	against	towards

1. The last post was collected _____ seven o'clock.

2. Did you arrive _____ train?

3. I felt unwell _____ the journey.

4. The monkeys climbed _____ the tree trunk to get to the food.

5. When you went to the cinema, who did you go _____?

6. Dad found the book we had been looking_____.

7. The lorry drove _____ the tunnel then _____ the bridge.

8. We walked _____ the towpath _____ we got tired.

9. The audience waited _____ the play _____ begin.

10. The footpath started _____ the lake and finished _____ the castle.

Read the following sentences and select the best preposition from the ones in brackets.
On another sheet of paper, write each sentence again with the preposition you have chosen.

1. The new road bridge went (beneath/across) the river.

2. (behind/between) our school and the church is a football pitch.

3. Always wash your hands (before/after) eating and brush your teeth (before/after) every meal.

4. My dad fell asleep (during/until) the film.

5. (by/at) four o'clock the party will begin.

6. I can go shopping (for/with) you as you are not feeling very well, Grandad.

7. I practised my catching by throwing a ball (against/towards) the garage doors.

Apostrophe to show possession

Add apostrophes of possession to each sentence below where they are needed.

1. Serenas bedroom needed tidying.
2. The books and crayons were Davids.
3. The two teams changing rooms were locked when they arrived.
4. The visitors car park was full when we got there.
5. The dogs kennels and the horses stables were brand new.
6. All of the womens clothes are next to the mens shoes.
7. His car was parked near Rebeccas.
8. Daniels case was packed ready for a weeks holiday.
9. The art gallerys new extension was opened by the Mayors wife.
10. My friends house is bigger than my uncles.

On another sheet of paper, write out the following sentences putting in the missing capital letters for all the proper nouns.

1. captain cook's ship the endeavour sailed to australia and tahiti.
2. My best friend, shane, is martin's brother.
3. The church of st. peter's is in walker road.
4. The first film in the lord of the rings series won several oscars last year.
5. dick king-smith has written many children's books including the bestseller the sheep pig, which was made into a film called babe.
6. The grand national is one of the most famous horse races in the world.
7. The people of switzerland speak several languages including german and french.
8. If I won the lottery I would buy a jaguar car and a villa in spain.
9. My uncle george and aunty mary live in yorkshire, near bradford.
10. The prime minister and president of america met at a conference held in northern ireland.

Helpful hints for writing a persuasive formal letter

✦ Remember the purpose of persuasive writing is to persuade the reader to accept your point of view.

✦ Plan your letter carefully.

✦ Try to seem reasonable and be polite.

✦ Try to be impersonal and use formal language.

✦ Put your arguments across clearly and in a logical order.

Structuring your text

✦ Begin by clearly stating your position or idea.

✦ Follow this with a series of points that support your opening argument. Try to make the points in a logical order so that they flow from one to another.

✦ Expand on some of these points and give facts and evidence in support of what you are saying.

✦ Write a separate paragraph for each point.

✦ Finish by writing a concluding paragraph that restates your position and summarises your main points.

Language features

✦ Try to sound reasonable to show you have thought out why you have taken this view point or position.

✦ Use phrases such as:

Everybody agrees that …

We all know that …

It is well known that…

Undoubtedly it …

Emotional language

✦ Use emotional language to try to influence the reader. Use emotive phrases such as:

I can assure you…

You will be aware…

We feel this most strongly…

A desirable outcome would be…

Formal letters

✦ Remember that a formal letter is written for a specific purpose and is usually addressed to a representative of an organisation.

✦ If you know the name of the person you are writing to then address them by it. If you do not know the name of the person you are writing to then use the standard form:

Dear Sir or Madam

✦ Use an impersonal style:

I am writing in response to your letter of the 31st March.

✦ Put your own address in the top right-hand corner. Put the address of recipient on the left-hand side one line below your own address.

✦ Use separate paragraphs for each point you wish to make.

✦ End your letter with a formal ending.

Yours faithfully (if the name of the recipient is unknown).

Yours sincerely (if name of recipient is known).

Formal letter
Scaffold 1

You are going to write a formal letter to your headteacher to persuade him/her to allow you to hold a charity event at school.

To help you write your letter, use the framework below.

Choose one option from each stage or use your own ideas.

Stage One

Choose one of the following charity events:

a) a jumble sale;
b) talent show;
c) sponsored walk.

Stage Two

Decide on the following:

- the charity you are supporting, the work they do and why you want to support them;
- when and where you want to hold your event;
- how you will organise your event;
- what you want from the school – use of hall/grounds/space for advertising the event/use of school paper/materials and so on.

Stage Three

Begin your letter with 'Dear (headteacher's name)' and write your opening paragraph. State clearly why you are writing.

a) I am writing to request that…
b) I am writing to seek your support in the matter of…
c) I am writing on the behalf of… with regard to holding an event to support their work.

Stage Four

Use the next paragraphs to give more details.

a) This charity is very important to me because…

b) This charity has worked so hard to help others that I think we as a school should try and help also. Therefore I think we should…

c) In our school assemblies you often tell us about how important it is to help others so I thought this would be an ideal opportunity for the whole school to…

Stage Five

What response do you want to your letter?

a) You would like the headteacher to write back to you with a favourable reply.

b) You hope the headteacher will agree that the charity is worth supporting.

c) You hope that the headteacher will appreciate the effort you put into writing the letter and will agree to the charity event.

d) You would like to arrange for a representative from the charity to visit the school so the headteacher can make an informed decision about holding the event.

HEAD TEACHER

Stage Six

Sum up your letter and sign off.

WHICH ENDING WILL I CHOOSE?

a) So you can see, this is a very important charity and I hope you will agree to go ahead.

b) I hope that I may be able to organise this event so that our school can help others.

c) I really hope that you will agree to this event.

Yours sincerely,
(sign your name)

Formal letter
Vocabulary bank 1

appreciate
assistance
benefit
charity
collect
collection
conclusion
consider
draw your attention to
encourage
essential
event
fund raising
furthermore

good cause
grateful
help others
I await your reply
I can assure you
I look forward to
   hearing from you
in addition
kindness
on behalf of
organise
permission
persuade
raise money for

really think
reply
request
responsible
school
seek your support
sponsorship
suggestion
therefore
trust
valuable
welcome your
   response

My own words

Formal letter
Scaffold 2

You are going to write a formal letter to try and persuade the local council to respond to your point of view.

To help you write your letter, use the framework below.

Choose one option from each stage.

Stage One

Choose one of the following to write your letter about:

a) the playground in your local park is in a terrible condition and needs repair;

b) the local council is planning to close the youth club held at your school;

c) a new factory has been built near your school and there is an increase in traffic on the road outside your school.

Set out your letter in the correct way:

1 Write your own address in the top right-hand corner;

2 Write the date underneath;

3 Address your letter to: Mr I Sore, Councillor, Local Council Chambers, High St, New Town, NT12 9GE. Write this under the date on the left-hand side.

Stage Two

Decide what your position on the matter is and what you want to persuade the council to do.

a) Do you want the playground to be closed or repaired? Should it be completely rebuilt? Should it be made larger? Should it be moved? What do you want the council to do?

b) Should the youth club close? Should it be kept? Should it be open more often or less often? Should it be held elsewhere? What do you want the council to do?

c) Has the road become more dangerous? Is there a need for new road safety measures? Are school children in danger? What do you want the council to do?

Stage Three

Begin your letter with 'Dear Mr Sore' and write your opening paragraph. State clearly why you are writing.

a) I am writing to express my concern over…
b) I am writing in response to your article about…
c) It has been brought to my attention that…
d) I am writing to seek your support in the matter of…
e) I am writing on the behalf of… with regard to the matter of…

Stage Four

Use the next paragraphs to give more details.

a) This playground has been part of our town for over 20 years now and I am really concerned that it is only now that it has fallen into disrepair. Only last week…
b) Very few towns have a lively youth club where children can go to enjoy themselves, happy in the knowledge that they are safely looked after so/but…
c) Many people in the town now have a job at the new factory near our school so I am really pleased that it has been built but I need to point out several issues to you.

Stage Five

What response do you want to your letter?

a) You want the council to respond immediately to solve the situation.
b) You want the council to arrange a meeting so everyone can put forward their views.
c) You want the councillor to visit the site to carry out a survey.
d) You want the council to put up safety barriers/keep the club open until the problem has been solved.

Stage Six

Sum up your letter and sign off.

a) I hope that my complaint will be taken seriously and that the council will…
b) I sincerely hope that the council will provide a quick and simple solution to the problem. I await your reply.
c) So you can see, the situation cannot be ignored and I hope to receive a prompt reply from you soon.
Yours sincerely,
(sign your name)

Formal letter
Vocabulary bank 2

accident
alarmed
amenity
appalled
before it's too late
campaign
community
conclusion
dangerous
decision
encourage
environment
express my concern
facility

families
for example
furthermore
harmful
hopeful
however
in response to
neighbourhood
on behalf of
oppose
pedestrian
persuade
public
repair

resource
safety
seek your support
service
solution
strongly
therefore
urge you to
valuable
vehicle
with regard to
worried

My own words

Should animals be kept in zoos?

Every year 350 million people visit nearly 750 zoos across the world. Humans have a natural curiosity about animals and zoos provide an opportunity to see animals from around the world close up and find out more about them.

However, some people believe that keeping animals in captivity is wrong and is cruel to the animals and that the public can learn about animals through television and other means.

In contrast, people who defend zoos argue that one of their most important functions is to raise public awareness about wildlife. Many zoos are involved in scientific research and conservation projects because they claim that without these projects many animals would become extinct if they were left solely in the wild.

Humans have kept animals in captivity for thousands of years. The old idea of a zoo was simply a collection of animals to be stared at as a curiosity. Little, if any, thought was given to the conditions they were kept in. Their surroundings were often bare and cramped with little thought given to what the animals needed to encourage their natural behaviour in the wild. The animals became confused, bored and frustrated and often behaved in ways that they would not have done if they had been living in their natural habitat. However, nowadays zoos have very different ideas about how they should operate and care for the welfare of their animals.

Consequently, the best zoos today put the welfare of the animals before the needs of visitors. They are kept in specially-designed cages and enclosures which recreate as close as possible their natural environment. For instance: animals that like to climb are provided with trees, branches and climbing frames; animals that burrow have banks of earth in which to explore and build homes. In this way, visitors have the opportunity to see animals behave more like they would in the wild.

Furthermore, many of the best zoos do not capture animals in the wild but have a breeding programme which means that the animals born in captivity do not have to make the enormous adjustment from life in the wild to life in captivity. Forty years ago only about 36 per cent of the captive animals were born in zoos, now the figure is nearer 75 per cent. Some of the animals bred in captivity are very rare and are close to extinction in the wild. Zoos argue that without these breeding programmes some of these species would die out. Colin Rawlings of the Zoological Society of London argues that, 'Ultimately zoos may provide the last refuge for the many species of animals that face extinction in the wild.' An example of this is the Père David's deer which has been saved from extinction through being bred in zoos.

In addition, the best zoos not only breed animals in captivity but try to reintroduce them back into their natural habitat. This is very difficult to do and is not always successful. Where this has been successful supporters of zoos say it is because of the knowledge zoos have of the animals and their needs, and that this knowledge is shared with other scientists and conservationists working in the wild. Scientists working in zoos are able to work closely with the animals and learn what they need to maintain good health, breed, survive and thrive in their natural habitats. This knowledge is then shared with other scientists all over the world. Zoos are just one part of a worldwide programme of conservation.

It is not only other scientists who benefit from this knowledge – the general public also learns more about the needs and lives of these creatures through information about the animals being displayed, lectures given and multi-media displays. The zoos hope that this will encourage the public to support

wildlife projects, such as the World Wide Fund for Nature, Greenpeace and Friends of the Earth.

Nevertheless, opponents of zoos believe that zoos mainly teach the public about the captive behaviour of animals and that many zoos around the world have little, if any, educational value at all. They contend that the best zoos use teaching methods that do not require live animals at all. They use modern technology to teach visitors and do not require the physical presence of the zoo animals. Because of the popularity of television programmes about wildlife, the public are more aware of how animals behave in the wild and when they visit zoos they recognise that the behaviour these animals display is not always natural.

Organisations like Born Free and Zoo Check say that zoos show a distorted picture of wild animals, claiming that the animals often live in unnatural conditions, display unnatural behaviour and are merely caricatures of the animal in the wild. Bill Travers of Zoo Check claims, 'Animals in captivity suffer from stress and, like humans, they can also die from it.' Wild animals lead complex and unpredictable lives – each species has evolved in such a way as to meet the challenges of its environment. As a consequence, traditional zoos can do little to reproduce this properly with their animal exhibits.

Zoo Check estimates that there are more than five million animals held in zoos worldwide and that their conditions vary from total impoverishment and deprivation to improved facilities, where some effort is made to reduce the stresses that result from captivity.

Despite these better zoos' attempts to provide more suitable enclosures and cages, some people believe there is no such thing as an ideal zoo and that animals in captivity will always suffer from lack of freedom.

The argument that some of these animals would become extinct if they were not kept in zoos is countered by opponents of zoos. Many zoos proclaim an interest and contribution to conservation but only a few actually keep and breed endangered species. Most zoo animals are not endangered and are the species that have the most public appeal. Less glamorous creatures are rarely kept.

As for zoos that claim to assist the release of animals back into the wild, their opponents argue that they are rarely successful and the cost is enormous. They contend that it is much less expensive to do this through programmes based in the animal's actual environment – such as game reserves and national parks – and these are considerably more successful.

One of the reasons that they are more successful is that the research undertaken by scientists in the wild is focused on the animal's natural behaviour and welfare not on their behaviour and needs in captivity. Opponents of zoos agree that the research done in zoos does have value but generally concentrates on the study of disease and anatomy, and is mainly aimed at keeping the animals in captivity and therefore is of limited value to scientists in the wild.

In conclusion, many zoos have improved and look after the animals much better than in the past. Most no longer capture animals in the wild but instead breed them in captivity. They attempt to recreate the animals' natural environment as best they can so they are as contented as possible. Undoubtedly some species have been saved from extinction through breeding programmes and the care of the few remaining animals left alive.

On the other hand, even the best zoos cannot replicate the exact natural environment of its animals. The creatures are still captives and deprived of their freedom and the choice to live as they choose. The public is more educated about conservation through the media and is beginning to question the value and role of zoos. The money spent on running zoos could instead be used to support larger and more extensive conservation programmes in the natural habitats of the captive creatures. And finally, the research undertaken by zoos could be transferred to these projects.

Understanding the grammar and punctuation

Connectives

Connectives are words or phrases that join one sentence or paragraph to another. They make the writing flow more smoothly.

<u>However</u>, nowadays zoos have very different...

<u>Consequently</u>, the best zoos today put...

Connectives are also used to link clauses within sentences. They can be conjunctions such as *but, when* and *because* or connecting adverbs such as *however, then* and *therefore*.

Many zoos proclaim an interest and contribution to conservation <u>but</u> only a few actually keep and breed endangered species.

Many zoos are involved in scientific research and conservation projects <u>because</u> they claim that without these projects many animals would become extinct if they were left solely in the wild.

Punctuating complex sentences

Punctuation is important within longer more complex sentences.
Commas are used to mark the beginning and end of clauses.

Opponents of zoos agree that the research done in zoos does have some value, although it generally concentrates on the study of disease and anatomy, but it is mainly aimed at keeping the animals in captivity and therefore is of limited value to scientists in the field.

Commas are also used to mark off connecting adverbs or adverbial phrases or clauses:

As a consequence, traditional zoos can do little to properly reproduce this with their animal exhibits.

Other punctuation can be used, for instance a **dash**.

Wild animals lead complex and unpredictable lives – each species has evolved to ideally meet the challenges of its environment.

The writer, however, could equally have used a **semicolon** (;)

Wild animals lead complex and unpredictable lives; each species has evolved to ideally meet the challenges of its environment.

Connectives

Complete each of the following sentences by adding one of the
connectives from the box below with your own words.

1. The team played well _____

    _____

2. The climber scaled the first ridge_____

    _____

3. The bustling market was one of the town's attractions_____

    _____

4. The holiday resort was smaller than we had expected_____

    _____

5. The car park was full_____

    _____

6. The demonstrators marched noisily along the street_____

    _____

7. The children were sent to the headteacher_____

    _____

8. The museum was being refurbished_____

    _____

9. There was a variety of classes at the college_____

    _____

10. The gardens attached to the stately home_____

    _____

but	when	because	however	then	therefore
nevertheless	meanwhile	consequently	moreover		

Write sentences for any connectives you have not used.

Name

Punctuating complex sentences

All the punctuation has been taken out of the following text. Rewrite it putting in the punctuation and organising it into paragraphs.

it is a sticky issue that has troubled generations of ice lolly lovers how do you eat one in the sun without it dripping on to your fingers now it seems scientists have it licked they say they have come up with a formula for the non-melting lolly claimed as a world first its special blend means it doesn't drip or dissolve according to supermarket chain ice cave instead when the strawberry lolly is removed from the freezer and begins to defrost it turns slowly into a fruit jelly as a result it maintains its shape around the stick david smith ice caves spokesman said we have listened to our customers who have said they love ice lollies for the kids but hate the sticky mess that comes with them the non drip lolly has been tried out on a number of consumers including a group of manchester primary schoolchildren their verdict was positive

_____

_____

_____

_____

_____

_____

_____

_____

_____

_____

Continue on the back of this sheet.

Helpful hints for writing a discussion text

Research

✦ Research the issue and gather information and viewpoints from both sides of the argument. Use a variety of sources, such as:

- books;
- magazines;
- leaflets;
- the Internet;
- interviews with individuals.

✦ Remember – Internet sources may be biased and present an unbalanced view so take care when using them.

✦ Make notes and use a paragraph plan to organise them. For instance, a simple way of organising arguments for and against is to use a grid plan.
- Points and evidence
- Arguments for
- Arguments against

Organising your writing

✦ Use the following standard structure.

- Begin with an opening paragraph which introduces the subject and then include some background to it so as to put it into context.

- Use the next paragraph to give a clear summary of the two opposing arguments.

- Use the following paragraphs to present one side of the argument, each dealing with a specific point. Support these points with evidence.

- Use the next paragraphs to present points to counter the argument presented previously.

- Use the final paragraph or two final paragraphs to give a summary of both sides' arguments, leaving the reader to reach their own conclusion.

Support the arguments in a variety of ways

✦ Present facts and statistics.

✦ Use quotes from important people or official sources.

✦ Provide specific examples.

✦ Use your own experience.

✦ Appeal to the audience's opinions.

Language features

✦ Try to connect ideas logically and to present your points clearly and precisely.

Avoid using:
- emotive language;
- exaggeration;
- illogical arguments;
- abusive language;
- statistics that don't really say anything or could be misunderstood.

Discussion writing
Scaffold 1

You are going to write a discussion text about the following issue: Do children watch too much television?

To help you write your discussion, use the framework below.

Choose one option from each stage.

Stage One

Research the subject by asking friends, parents and other adults for their views and the reasons they hold them.

Find out the following:

a) Ask your friends how much television they watch each day / each week.

b) What sort of programmes do they watch? (entertainment, sport, music, soaps, magazine-type programmes, educational programmes such as documentaries, news programmes)

c) When do they watch television?

d) What would they be doing if they didn't have a television or were not watching television?

Use the Internet to find out what other people think.

Make notes on your findings.

Make notes of what they say and add your own ideas.

Stage Three

Use your research notes to make a paragraph plan like this:

Paragraph:

1. Introduction.

2. Background information about the issue.

3. Key points for (Yes, children DO watch too much television).

4. Key points against (No, children DO NOT watch too much television).

5. Conclusion – a summary of main arguments for both sides.

Stage Three

Write your opening paragraph.
Introduce the topic and give a brief background to the issue.
You could begin like this:

a) Television is the most popular from of media today, especially for children.

b) Over 80 per cent of homes in the UK have a television set.

c) Television has become very popular with viewers of all ages.

d) Television can entertain, inform and educate.

Stage Four

Write your second and third paragraphs. This will briefly outline the main arguments for each side.

Choose one of these openings to write the case FOR:

a) Supporters of the argument that…(write in your issue) argue that…

b) The case for… is based on…

c) The main argument in support of… is…

d) Supporters of… believe that…

e) Advocates of the case for… claim that…

Choose one of these openings to write the case AGAINST:

a) However, opponents believe that…

b) On the other hand some people argue that…

c) Opponents counter this by stating…

d) The counter argument is that…

e) The main argument against… is…

Stage Five

Now write your concluding paragraph. This should summarise the main argument for and against the issue.

Start with a phrase like:

a) In conclusion, many people believe that…

b) In short people who believe children do watch too much television believe…

c) So it can be seen that…

d) This contentious issue continues to be discussed with defenders claiming…

Discussion writing
Vocabulary bank 1

advantages
argue
argument
because
benefits
boredom
children
conclusion
consequently
conversation
disadvantages
educational
entertainment

eventually
every
family
great
habits
hours
however
interesting
moreover
nevertheless
opponents
programmes
solution

television
therefore
too much
uninteresting
valuable
value
viewing
views
watches
young

My own words

Discussion writing
Scaffold 2

You are going to write a discussion text which presents arguments from both sides of an issue.

To help you write your discussion, use the framework below.

Choose one option from each stage.

Stage One

Choose one of the following issues to write about:

a) Should girls/females be allowed to play football with boys/males?

b) Should girls and boys be taught in separate classes or schools?

c) Should the school day be made longer?

d) Should schools be open on Saturdays?

Gather views and information about your chosen subject. Talk to your friends, teachers, parents and other people and ask them for their own opinions and reasons for them.

Carry out further research using a variety of sources. Use books, CD-Roms and the Internet.

Stage Two

Write your opening paragraph.
Introduce the topic and give a brief background to the issue.
You could begin like this:

a) There has been some debate for several years as to whether or not girls should be allowed to play football with boys.

b) Would boys' school results be improved if they were taught in separate classes to girls?

c) The length of the school day has long been an issue for discussion.

d) Many independent schools have their schools open on a Saturday. Should state schools follow suit?

Stage Three

Write your second paragraph. This will briefly outline the main arguments for each side.

Choose one of these openings.
a) Supporters of the argument that… (write in your issue) argue that…
b) The case for… is based on….
c) The main argument in support of… is…
d) Supporters of… believe that…
e) Advocates of the case for… claim that…

The second half of this paragraph will outline the opposing views.
Use phrases like:
a) However, opponents believe that…
b) On the other hand some people argue that…
c) Opponents counter this by stating…
d) The counter argument is that…
e) The main argument against… is…

Stage Four

Now write your next paragraphs.

Each paragraph should focus on one point at a time and be backed up with evidence.
Use quotes from organisations, individuals and important people.
Present the argument for the issue first, then counter this by writing a paragraph which deals with the same point but from the other side's view point.

Link the two paragraphs for each point by using linking phrases like:

a) Nevertheless opponents counter this by…
b) However, this view is not held by everyone.
c) The opposing view, however, believes…
d) On the other hand…
e) Although this view is held by some, there are many people who believe that…

Stage Five

Now write your concluding paragraph. This should summarise the main argument for and against the issue.

Start with a phrase like:
a) In conclusion, many people believe that…
b) In short defenders of the case for… state…
c) So it can be seen that…
d) This contentious issue continues to be discussed with defenders claiming…

Discussion writing
Vocabulary bank 2

advantages
against
although
argue
argument
believe
benefits
competition
consequently
convince
defend

discussed
equal
equality
examination
female
however
in conclusion
information
issue
male
nevertheless

opposite
point of view
pros and cons
results
safety
Saturday
separate
summary
support
therefore

My own words